I0820095

ASIAN SMOKE

ASIAN SMOKE

THAI AND SOUTHEAST ASIAN BARBECUE FROM THE CURRY BOYS

ANDREW HO, ANDREW SAMIA, AND SEAN WEN

Quarto.com

First Published in 2026 by The Harvard Common Press, an imprint of The Quarto Group,
100 Cummings Center, Suite 265-D, Beverly, MA 01915, USA.
T (978) 282-9590 F (978) 283-2742

EEA Representation, WTS Tax d.o.o.,
Žanova ulica 3, 4000 Kranj, Slovenia.
www.wts-tax.si

The Harvard Common Press titles are also available at discount for retail, wholesale, promotional, and bulk purchase. For details, contact the Special Sales Manager by email at specialsales@quarto.com or by mail at The Quarto Group, Attn: Special Sales Manager, 100 Cummings Center, Suite 265-D, Beverly, MA 01915, USA.

30 29 28 27 26 1 2 3 4 5

ISBN: 978-1-57715-641-3

Digital edition published in 2026
eISBN: 978-1-57715-642-0

Library of Congress Cataloging-in-Publication Data available

Design and Page Layout: Emily Austin, The Sly Studio
Photography: Eric Pohl with food styling by Susan Gebhard, except Beef Loving Texans on page 248
Illustration: Shutterstock

Printed in Guangdong, China TT122025

THIS BOOK IS *DEDICATED TO*

the BBQ community that has unconditionally welcomed us and embraced us, to the Asian community who constantly inspires us to be proud and true to ourselves, and to everyone who has ever supported us throughout the years. You have our absolute deepest gratitude.

CONTENTS

CHAPTER 4

ON THE SIDE

CHAPTER 5

SEAFOOD AND VEGGIE MAINS

CHAPTER 6

CHICKEN AND DUCK MAINS

LONE
STAR

CHAPTER 7

BRISKET AND OTHER BEEF MAINS

CHAPTER 8

PORK AND LAMB MAINS

CHAPTER 9

SWEETS AND DESSERTS

PREFACE

AUTHENTICALLY ASIAN, AUTHENTICALLY AMERICAN

by Sean Wen, cofounder and co-owner, Curry Boys BBQ

How the hell did we get here? Never in a million years did the three of us imagine we would have an opportunity to write a cookbook about Asian-inspired Texas barbecue, the food we love. And while I still think this might be some cruel, incredibly drawn-out April Fool's joke, this opportunity truly is a testament to the talent of our trusty pitmaster, Andrew Samia, and the absolute moxie of our chief flavor officer, Andrew Ho. I'm so grateful I get to work with these two jokers, and I feel so lucky to be a part of such an incredible and welcoming barbecue community.

Speaking of Texas barbecue, I can still vividly remember when Andrew Ho changed my life by introducing me to Aaron Franklin's barbecue. This was back when Franklin's was still a food truck posted up along Interstate 35 in a random lot off the highway in Austin. It was early 2010, and I was a young, bright-eyed college student who cared about only two things: eating at "dope" spots and playing insane amounts of basketball. In fact, there was a moment in my life where I legitimately thought I was going to "make it to the League." Hilarious, I know, but I digress. With a crumpled twenty-dollar bill and a handful of quarters that I "borrowed" from our communal dorm laundry room, Andrew and I pulled up to the dusty lot next to Franklin's, excited to taste something so legendary that years later people would literally describe it as the "best brisket in the world."

After waiting anxiously for 45 minutes in a line where we saw happy guest after happy guest walk past us with a platter of perfectly smoked meats, and with the lingering smell of post oak smoke filling the air around us, we finally shuffled to the front. My eyes darted around, looking at the menu, doing quick math in my head to see if the money I had scrounged up was enough for what I wanted to order. It was like that scene in *The Hangover* where Zach Galifianakis's character is at the blackjack table and sees numbers and equations literally floating around him, except that instead of calculating the probability of cards, I was calculating brisket prices, the costs of adding sides, and the exact amount of sales tax I would owe. All of a sudden, the truck window squeaked closed and I saw a man awkwardly fastening a little sign to the window: "Sold Out." My heart sank. There was no way. Aaron Franklin had *just* sold out in front of my freaking eyeballs. I couldn't believe it. I remember looking at Andrew and telling him I'd rather fail a final exam, potentially dishonoring my family, than feel this way. He laughed wryly, rolled his eyes at me, and let out an exasperated

536
536
E COURTLAND
BUSINESS
HOURS:
PUSH
Welcome
to
Curry
Boys

sigh. Alas, our dreams of a succulent, slow-smoked BBQ feast were dashed, replaced by the grim reality of a gas station taquito and a fountain soda the size of my face. As we began to walk away, we heard a voice and the sound of the window sliding back open. I spun back around and that's when I saw him. Like a goddamn angel peering through parted clouds, it was Aaron Franklin's unmistakable face, glasses slightly crooked above a smile so genuine, it would probably melt Cruella de Vil's ice-cold heart.

"Really sorry we sold out, but do you guys want a couple brisket burnt ends and leftover brisket bits? It's on the house, guys!"

I must have blacked out from the instant relief and excitement after hearing this, because I don't recall the trip back. I just remember somehow teleporting back to my small room and eating some of the best food I'd ever eaten at this point in my life. I was in heaven. The brisket melted. The smokiness of the bark lingered. The soft, milky, white bread was pure nostalgic joy. I vividly remember this moment and how badly I wished I could be a part of this barbecue world, one way or another. The allure was undeniable: smoking meats, building layers of flavor, and ultimately, selling a legendary experience. However, what sticks out even more in my memory of that moment was an overwhelming sense of intimidation and the overall sense that this would probably be another pipe dream, much like my misaligned hoop dreams. There just wasn't a chance that an Asian American nerd who played cello in middle school, had an above-average jump shot, and played World of Warcraft on the weekends was ever going to be welcomed in the barbecue community. There weren't too many Asian chefs to begin with, let alone Asians who were connected to the Texas barbecue world. It just wasn't "traditionally" seen, and I worried it probably wouldn't ever look or feel "authentic."

This brings me to the idea of authenticity, or possibly the lack thereof, which is really the backbone of this cookbook. There are more people than ever in the food and beverage industry embracing the idea that "authentic food" is simply food that is an authentic expression of themselves and their unique life stories that marry multiple cultures, rather than the mimicking of one culture's historic food references and traditions. It's this type of anecdotal authenticity, made up from personal stories and lived experiences, that is finally being sought after and admired in the industry, and it has excitingly made its way to Texas barbecue. Luckily, as the accessibility of learning the secrets of smoking meat has skyrocketed in the past ten years, so too has the idea of incorporating different cultures into what is classically known as "traditional Texas barbecue."

Texas barbecue is not a monolith, and it shouldn't be. As more and more first-generation immigrants learn how to smoke meat, they inevitably take their favorite dishes, flavors, and spices and pour them into the art of barbecue. This is how things evolve; how flavors continue leveling up. Most importantly, this is how people can become more open-minded to new

cultures and willing to try new culinary ideas. When things are done strictly traditionally, society tends to pigeon-hole a culture into a single niche, a single idea. And while I think acknowledging, valuing, and honoring tradition are still extremely important in many regards, doing *only* that does not leave any room for the idea of novelty or of trying new things. It does not leave room for food cultures to change and evolve, as they must. And it certainly leaves little room for individual creativity and expression.

While many of the Texas barbecue techniques in this book are done traditionally, the unique flavors and different ideas that we impart are done in a natural and meaningful way because they were, and still are, a part of our actual lives. I can remember as a teenager sitting around the dinner table with stir-fried bok choy, marinated tofu, a bowl of perfectly cooked rice, and a big bucket of Church's fried chicken. Hell yes. This was a normal dinner—expected, even. My immigrant dad absolutely adored fried chicken, gulf shrimp, and BBQ, while my mother was what I like to affectionately call "an ardent supporter of the Asian culinary arts." (She only ever cooked Chinese food, but damn, was it good!) I cherished both cultures as I grew up, and a world without either would feel barren and incomplete. Andrew Ho, for his part, spent three years of his life living in Thailand and Vietnam, eating his way through those cuisines, reconnecting with his cultural roots, yet still holding dear his Texan upbringing.

This book is not about forcing two different cultures together for the sake of going viral online or for the shock effect. We aren't sitting in a lab concocting two parts Asian to one part Texas—trying to find the perfect scientific balance between the two. We aren't scouring some list on Buzzfeed like, "18 Food Trends Older People Grew Up With That Will Sound Totally Bizarre to Kids These Days" (yes, that is an actual article title) to find nostalgic recipes that would instantly become a hit on the Internet. The recipes in this book are just simply some of our favorite dishes to cook, and they just happen to be inspired by Asia and Texas—two cultures we respect and love equally. Many of these recipes actually come from Curry Boys BBQ, a restaurant founded in October 2020 by me and my close friends, Andrew Ho and Andrew Samia. The concept is Thai curry meets Texas barbecue, but at its core, Curry Boys is the beautiful amalgamation of three individuals, our unique perspectives, and ultimately, our expression of what we enjoy smoking, cooking, and eating! And honestly, that is what we want you to take away from this book: to unapologetically be yourself when it comes to smoking and barbecuing. As long as you respect the craft and the cultures, you're free to make the food your own.

(Speaking of "unapologetically being yourself," as I write this, I legitimately have a basketball game in an hour. As always, I'm going to convince myself that this will be my breakout game and that an NBA scout will be there by chance to tell me I should try out for a team. I wish I was lying. Anyway, I'll probably see you guys in the NBA—or at Curry Boys BBQ eating some Asian-inspired Texas barbecue. Either way, I won't apologize for being me.)

A SOUTHEAST ASIAN BARBECUE PANTRY AND A CONCISE GUIDE TO BARBECUE ESSENTIALS

YOUR SOUTHEAST ASIAN BARBECUE PANTRY

Cooking Southeast Asian–inspired food may seem daunting and bewildering to some folks. I promise you it is actually quite easy—as long as you are prepared. Luckily, most Asian supermarkets or grocery stores will carry these pantry items, and once you stock your kitchen or pantry, you'll be well on your way to achieving culinary greatness! And if not "greatness," at least you'll be able to cook the recipes in this cookbook. So, here's to shooting for the culinary moon and knowing you'll at least fall somewhere amongst the Southeast Asian–inspired stars.

★ **Fish sauce:** The lifeblood of Southeast Asian cuisine—primarily in Thai, Laotian, Cambodian, and Vietnamese cooking. We love using Squid—a Thai brand—for everyday use because it isn't too expensive, is widely accessible, and has the perfect amount of funk. It tends to be a bit on the saltier side compared with other fish sauces, so use it in moderation; a little goes a long way!

★ **Palm sugar:** Typically coming in the form of a block or a puck, palm sugar is a popular Thai ingredient when it comes to desserts and adding a unique touch of sweetness to a dish. It has a distinct caramel-like flavor, and unlike white granulated sugar, is a bit more complex and nuanced. To use palm sugar, you can finely chop it, or if it is too hard to cut, you can use a mortar and pestle. Finely chopped palm sugar weighs about 12 grams per tablespoon. You can substitute brown sugar for palm sugar if necessary.

★ **Bird's Eye chili (Thai chili):** Southeast Asian countries *love* spice and heat. We love these Thai chilies because they pack a punch and are slightly fruity and peppery! Red ones are ripe, earthy, and have a more mellow flavor. Green ones are underripe, less spicy, and more herbaceous.

★ **Lemongrass:** This essential, citrus-smelling herb is found all over Southeast Asia and used primarily for its aromatic nature. It is used in so many recipes because of its versatility and signature ability to brighten up any dish.

- ★ **Fried shallots:** They're slightly sweet, provide a delightful crunch, and are a popular garnish for many Southeast Asian dishes. You can certainly make them at home, but we like going to the store and buying a big bag, because the quality of store-bought fried shallots is pretty great. You can always reheat them in the oven to toast them up a bit more if you'd like.
- ★ **Jasmine rice:** This fragrant type of rice is a staple in Southeast Asia. It's pillowy, fluffy, and has the perfect chew. The grain's length is somewhere in between basmati and short-grain sushi rice or rice you might find in East Asia, allowing it to be sticky, but not clumpy.
- ★ **Thai basil:** This is used in so many stir-fry and curry recipes that it goes without saying how important it is to have a bunch or two at all times. Thai basil has a "spicier" and more peppery flavor profile compared with Italian basil and can withstand high heat. When fried or cooked, it adds a beautiful complexity to any dish!
- ★ **Coconut milk:** Not to be confused with coconut cream, coconut milk is the liquid that is squeezed from the meat of a mature coconut. It is popular in Southeast Asia because of its dairy-free nature and coconut's abundance in this tropical region of the world. If you're looking to add a creaminess and subtle sweetness to a dish, then look no further. Our favorite brand is Chaokoh.
- ★ **Soy sauces:** The world of soy sauce gets incredibly complex and difficult to wrap your head around, so we'll keep it simple for you. Having a dark soy sauce and a thin, or regular, soy sauce is key to any pantry. Dark soy sauce is primarily used for coloring and is thick and concentrated, while a thin light or regular soy sauce is the multipurpose sauce that you're familiar with. Although Thai soy sauce brands are recommended, any Chinese or Japanese soy sauce (like Kikkoman) will do the trick. Just be sure to adjust recipes slightly to the soy sauce that you have—as soy sauce brands and types tend to differ in salt levels.
- ★ **Oyster sauce:** Although it originated in China, oyster sauce has made its way to its Southeast Asian siblings and can be found in many dishes all over the region now. It is slightly sweet, delightfully savory, and perfect for a marinade, a sauce, or a stir-fry. Contrary to its name, there are no actual oysters in the sauce. Its name comes from the briny liquid left over from boiling oysters!
- ★ **Sweet chili sauce:** This popular sauce can be used straight out of the bottle as a dipping sauce or combined with other ingredients to create complex and wonderful sauces and marinades. Because of its sweetness, it pairs really well with savory or fried foods. We love the Mae Ploy brand of this sauce—as it is readily available at most grocery stores!
- ★ **Curry pastes:** There are five types of curry paste you'll use in this book. Massaman curry is not spicy, but is loaded with South Asian and Indian flavors. Penang curry is subtly hot from red chilies, but the creaminess from ground peanut or mung bean sets it apart. Yellow curry is mild and semisweet. Red curry is the second spiciest due to the ground red chilies. Finally, green curry might be the most popular curry in Thailand. It is aromatic and is the spiciest from the fresh green chilies used. You might be surprised to hear that it is extremely common practice in Thailand to purchase curry paste rather than make it from scratch. You can buy Thai curry pastes at any Asian market, and they're great because of their consistency. We prefer Mae Ploy brand!

BARBECUE AND SMOKING ESSENTIALS

Look, smoking meat and cooking Texas barbecue isn't exactly the hardest thing in the world. There are some people who launch freakin' rockets into outer space—*that* is rocket science. BBQ is simply mastering a combination of fire and time. Despite the simplicity, a lot can still go wrong, and we recognize that cooking great BBQ requires a certain level of skill, experience, and moxie to understand the sometimes fickle intricacies of fire and smoke. This is why we created a guide detailing essential equipment and seasonings to help you build a solid BBQ foundation. It ain't much, but it's honest work.

Smoker Selection

There are different types of smokers.

★ **Offset smoker:** The number one essential of a Texas barbecue pitmaster is an offset smoker. This means a smoker with a firebox for burning wood or charcoal with a separate, offset (hence the name) horizontal cooking chamber. The smoker will also have a chimney or a stack at the opposite end of the firebox to create draw. As the fire burns in the firebox, the fire sucks in more fuel (oxygen) to create heat and smoke. The heat and smoke then enter into the cooking chamber and flow over the meat on the grates before escaping out of the stack.

★ **Vertical or drum smoker:** This smoker is usually in a large upright cabinet or metal drum. The fire source is at the bottom of the cabinet and the meat is on racks above the fire. As the fire burns, heat and smoke rise upward to vents in the top of the smoker. Because the fire is directly under the meat, your meat doesn't get the protection from the fire as in an offset smoker. This makes it important to be mindful of the proximity of your meat to the fire and not to let things burn from underneath. Many pitmasters prefer to smoke fat-side down when using a vertical smoker so that the fat side of the meat can shield the meat from the heat.

Grills

Smokers are perfect for cooking tough, dense cuts of meat over long periods of time to break down connective tissue and render collagen, making the meat tender and juicy. Some cuts of meat, however, just aren't designed for the low-and-slow cooking of a smoker. This is where a grill comes in. Sure, there are tons of nice fancy grills with all the bells and whistles out there, but even in its most primitive and basic form—a simple metal grate over a circle brick firepit loaded with burning charcoal—a live fire grill is the perfect way to get a high-heat sear on a rib eye or lamb chop.

Wood

Wood selection is critical in barbecuing. Whenever you're smoking meat, especially on a 13-plus-hour cook, such as with a brisket, it's essential to maintain clean fires throughout your cook. This means having a solid bed of coals to start, burning wood that's not too green (that is, fresh), and making sure your fire is getting proper airflow. Otherwise, you can end up with really heavy smoke that can impart a lot of unwanted bitter flavors to your meat.

★ **Post oak:** Post oak makes a mild, clean smoke. It is a favorite of pitmasters in central Texas. It has a lower density and is best for long cooks like brisket as it is not as overpowering as other woods. Post oak is prominent throughout the central and southeast United States.

★ **White oak:** Similar to post oak, white oak is great for when post oak is not available. White oak is widely distributed and available in more areas. It burns slightly hotter than post oak and is not as flavorful.

- ★ **Hickory:** Hickory is a classic wood choice of southern pitmasters, primarily where pork is cooked. It has a distinct, delicious aroma when burning, and it burns down exceptionally well for coals to use for grilling.
- ★ **Mesquite:** Mesquite has a very strong flavor profile. It has a high density and burns hot, so it's best when used for short cooks like chicken, or as coals for grilling steaks and chops. Some South Texan pitmasters have mastered the use of mesquite in longer cooks like brisket, but it is something that requires practice and skill as it can leave a bitter flavor if used incorrectly.
- ★ **Pecan:** Pecan is a solid, all-purpose wood that is prominent throughout the South. It has a similar density to post oak and burns similarly, but it has a sweeter flavor profile, making it a perfect choice with pork and lamb.

SEASONINGS

Most of a classic Texas barbecue rub is simply salt and pepper. Especially when cooking brisket, it is important not to overpower the natural flavors of the beef but to enhance them with salt, smoke, and black pepper.

We like to use larger granules in our rubs to create a deeper and crunchier bark, so we use coarse kosher salt and 16-mesh ground black pepper. The 16-mesh ground black pepper better matches the size of the kosher salt granules, so it's easier visually to tell the ratio of your rub and that it is properly mixed up.

With other pork, poultry, lamb, seafood, and even vegetables, you have much more space to get creative and introduce other spices and seasonings.

chapter
1

SAUCES
and
RUBS

Makes 2¼ QUARTS (2.1 L)

THREE THAI CURRY SAUCES

Aragorn, Legolas, and Gimli. Harry, Hermione, and Ron. Luke, Leia, and Han Solo. What do all of these things have in common? Besides the fact that they are all from beloved fictional universes, with each group composed of individuals with distinct personalities and skills who come together to face extraordinary challenges, and have journeys that are marked by camaraderie, conflict, and unwavering loyalty, making them unforgettable figures in the annals of storytelling (takes deep breath), they're also iconic trios. And speaking of iconic trios, let us introduce you to the most *iconic trio: Thai green curry, Thai red curry, and Thai yellow curry. Traditionally, these Thai curries are made with the same ingredients but use different colored chiles—which is what gives the curries their distinct colors and taste. Yellow curry is mild, earthy, and semisweet. Red curry is the second spiciest because of its dried red chilies and is incredibly versatile given its well-balanced ingredients. Green curry—arguably the most popular curry in Thailand—is aromatic and usually the spiciest, thanks to its fresh green chilies. We typically opt for using Thai curry pastes that you can buy at any Asian market because of the consistency that they offer. We prefer Mae Ploy brand! It is extremely common practice in Thailand to purchase these curry pastes as well—and many times even recommended. What elevates our curry recipes, however, is how we incorporate fresh ingredients and herbs into the pastes to add depth and complex flavors.*

THAI GREEN CURRY SAUCE

2 tablespoons (30 ml) vegetable oil
3 tablespoons (14 g) finely minced fresh lemongrass
4 cloves garlic, minced
5 tablespoons (75 g) Thai green curry paste
3 tablespoons (39 g) white sugar
¼ cup (60 ml) fish sauce
1 teaspoon chicken bouillon powder
4 cups (946 ml) water
4 cups (896 g) coconut milk

1. In a large saucepan, heat vegetable oil on low to medium heat.
2. Add minced lemongrass and garlic. Lightly sauté in oil for about 2 to 3 minutes until fragrant.
3. Add in green curry paste and mix well. Continue stirring for another 3 to 4 minutes until the paste becomes extremely aromatic.
4. Gradually add sugar while stirring to mix well. Allow mixture to caramelize slightly for 1 to 2 minutes until curry paste turns to a deep green color.
5. Add in fish sauce and chicken bouillon and combine well. Let simmer for 4 to 5 minutes over low heat.
6. Add water and coconut milk and turn heat to high.
7. Add in cooked vegetables of your choice while stirring and bring curry to a low simmer. The curry is ready. It goes great with fatty proteins because the herbaceousness cuts through and balances with the fat beautifully! Store in a covered container in the refrigerator for up to 1 week.

Pictured from left to right: Thai Yellow Curry Sauce (page 26), Thai Red Curry Sauce (page 27), Thai Green Curry Sauce (this page)

Makes 2¼ QUARTS (2.1 L)

THAI YELLOW CURRY SAUCE

2 tablespoons (30 ml) vegetable oil
3 tablespoons (14 g) finely minced fresh lemongrass
4 cloves garlic, minced
5 tablespoons (75 g) Thai yellow curry paste
3 tablespoons (39 g) white sugar
¼ cup (60 ml) fish sauce
1 teaspoon chicken bouillon powder
4 cups (946 ml) water
4 cups (896 g) coconut milk

1. In a large saucepan, heat vegetable oil on low to medium heat.
2. Add minced lemongrass and garlic. Lightly sauté in oil for about 2 to 3 minutes until fragrant.
3. Add in yellow curry paste and mix well. Continue stirring for another 3 to 4 minutes until the paste becomes extremely aromatic.
4. Gradually add sugar while stirring to mix well. Allow mixture to caramelize slightly for 1 to 2 minutes until curry paste turns a deep yellow color.
5. Add in fish sauce and chicken bouillon and combine well. Let simmer for 4 to 5 minutes over low heat.
6. Add water and coconut milk to the curry paste mixture and turn heat to high.
7. Add in cooked vegetables of your choice while stirring and bring curry to a low simmer. The curry is ready. It goes great with vegetarian substitutes, seafood, and poultry because of the velvety-ness of the turmeric in the yellow curry! Store in a covered container in the refrigerator for up to 1 week.

Makes 2¼ QUARTS (2.1 L)

THAI RED CURRY SAUCE

2 tablespoons (30 ml) vegetable oil
3 tablespoons (14 g) finely minced fresh lemongrass
4 cloves garlic, minced
5 tablespoons (75 g) Thai red curry paste
3 tablespoons (39 g) white sugar
¼ cup (60 ml) fish sauce
1 teaspoon chicken bouillon powder
4 cups (946 ml) water
4 cups (896 g) coconut milk

1. In a large saucepan, heat vegetable oil on low to medium heat.
2. Add minced lemongrass and garlic. Lightly sauté in oil for about 2 to 3 minutes until fragrant.
3. Add in red curry paste and mix well. Continue stirring for another 3 to 4 minutes until the paste becomes extremely aromatic.
4. Gradually add sugar while stirring to mix well. Allow mixture to caramelize slightly for 1 to 2 minutes until curry paste turns a deep red color.
5. Add in fish sauce and chicken bouillon and combine well. Let simmer for 4 to 5 minutes over low heat.
6. Add water and coconut milk to the curry paste mixture and turn heat to high. Add in cooked vegetables of your choice while stirring and bring curry to a low simmer. The curry is ready. Store in a covered container in the refrigerator for up to 1 week.

Makes 2¼ QUARTS (2.1 L)

THAI PENANG CURRY SAUCE

Although Penang curry isn't one of the three so-called typical curries (those are red, yellow, and green curry), it is just as popular and well loved. At Curry Boys, it is our second most popular curry because of the subtle heat from red chilies and the creaminess from the legumes (typically peanut, or mung bean if trying to avoid allergies). While it might be similar in color to red curry, the ground peanut or mung bean that is found in the paste is what really sets this apart from the rest of the classic curries.

- 2 tablespoons (30 ml) vegetable oil
- 3 tablespoons (14 g) finely minced fresh lemongrass
- 6 cloves garlic, minced
- 5 tablespoons (75 g) Thai Penang curry paste
- 3 tablespoons (39 g) white sugar
- ¼ cup (60 ml) fish sauce
- 1 teaspoon chicken bouillon powder
- 4 cups (946 ml) water
- 4 cups (896 g) coconut milk

1. In a large saucepan, heat vegetable oil on low to medium heat.
2. Add minced lemongrass and garlic. Lightly sauté in oil for about 2 to 3 minutes until fragrant.
3. Add in Penang curry paste and mix well. Continue stirring for another 3 to 4 minutes until the paste becomes extremely aromatic.
4. Gradually add sugar while stirring to mix well. Allow mixture to caramelize slightly for 1 to 2 minutes until curry paste turns to a deep red color.
5. Add in fish sauce and chicken bouillon and combine well. Let simmer for 4 to 5 minutes over low heat.
6. Add water and coconut milk to the Penang curry paste mixture and turn heat to high. Add in cooked vegetables of your choice while stirring and bring curry to a low simmer. The curry is ready. Store in a covered container in the refrigerator for up to 1 week.

Makes **2¼ QUARTS (2.1 L)**

MASSAMAN *CURRY SAUCE*

Did you know that in 2011, CNN ranked massaman curry as the number one most delicious food in the world? That's an absolutely bonkers fact that you can tell someone at a dinner party when you use this recipe and impress everyone around you. We genuinely do love this recipe though because of how thick, rich, and creamy this curry is compared to other Thai curries. Massaman has a mild, neutral spice level that's reminiscent of South Asian and Indian flavors, making it a great option for kids who may have a lower spice tolerance. When we make this recipe and let people know they're eating the number one most delicious food in the world, they always agree.

2 tablespoons (30 ml) vegetable oil
2 white onions, minced
3 tablespoons (14 g) finely minced fresh lemongrass
4 cloves garlic, minced
¼ cup (60 g) Thai massaman curry paste
2 tablespoons (26 g) white sugar
3 tablespoons (45 ml) fish sauce
1 teaspoon chicken bouillon powder
½ cup (130 g) creamy peanut butter
4 cups (946 ml) water
4 cups (896 g) coconut milk

1. In a large saucepan, heat vegetable oil on low to medium heat.
2. Add minced white onion and sauté until soft and a bit caramelized, about 7 to 10 minutes.
3. Add minced lemongrass and garlic. Lightly sauté in a saucepan for about 2 to 3 minutes until fragrant.
4. Add in massaman curry paste and mix well. Continue stirring for another 3 to 4 minutes until the paste becomes extremely aromatic.
5. Gradually add sugar while stirring to mix well. Allow mixture to caramelize slightly for 1 to 2 minutes until curry paste turns a deep brownish red color.
6. Add in fish sauce and chicken bouillon and combine well. Let simmer for 4 to 5 minutes over low heat.
7. Add peanut butter and stir until everything is combined nicely.
8. Add water and coconut milk to the mixture and turn heat to high.
9. Add in cooked vegetables of your choice while stirring and bring curry to a low simmer. The curry is ready. Store in a covered container in the refrigerator for up to 1 week.

Makes **1½ QUARTS (1.4 L)**

VIET-CAJUN GARLIC BUTTER SEAFOOD SAUCE

Have you ever seen seafood restaurants that have big bags of boiled seafood drowned in a hearty, garlicky sauce? This is our version of that sauce. It's slightly sweeter than your classic seafood boil garlic butter sauces, but we tend to enjoy a bit of a sweeter bite. It still packs a savory punch and a spicy kick, so if you're looking for a bold sauce to accompany any seafood, look no further. Balling on a budget? Just throw some of this sauce on white rice and you got yourself the snack of the century! If you have leftover sauce, don't toss it. We recommend using it when stir-frying—particularly if you're making fried rice—or when basting smoked or grilled meats.

½ pound (227 g) unsalted butter
2 cups (473 ml) orange juice
2 cups (473 ml) water
2½ tablespoons (15 g) Cajun or seafood boil seasoning
1 teaspoon chicken bouillon powder
½ cup (115 g) brown sugar
1 teaspoon cayenne pepper
1 teaspoon paprika powder
½ cup (75 g) minced fresh garlic

1. In a medium saucepan, turn heat to medium and add everything but the garlic. Mix well and bring to a boil.
2. Once the sauce is boiling, add minced garlic and let simmer on low heat for 2 minutes. Cut heat and your sauce is now ready to be tossed with your favorite seafood. It goes great with boiled seafood (shrimp, mussels, crabs, crawfish, clams, and so on) and white rice! Store in a covered container in the refrigerator for up to 1 week.

BBQ SAUCE

Makes 1 QUART (1 L)

COLBY'S *FAMOUS THAI*-TEXAS *LEMONGRASS* BBQ SAUCE

Every Saturday at Curry Boys BBQ, we serve pork ribs, and this is the legendary sauce that the ribs are basted in. This recipe is cultural exchange personified—harmoniously merging the East and the West. It's a new-school take on an old-school, traditional barbecue sauce recipe, and most importantly, it's one of our most dependable sauces at the restaurant. Shout-out to our amazing Chef Colby for coming up with this gem! We genuinely love and appreciate you! This sauce is also great to baste chicken and beef. You can find lemongrass powder at your local Asian market.

1½ cups (360 g) ketchup
1 cup (235 ml) apple cider vinegar
1 cup (150 g) brown sugar
⅓ cup (79 ml) low-sodium regular soy sauce
2 tablespoons (13 g) black pepper
1 tablespoon (9 g) garlic powder
1 tablespoon (7 g) onion powder
2 teaspoons lemongrass powder

1. In a medium saucepan over medium heat, combine ketchup, apple cider vinegar, brown sugar, and soy sauce. Stir and mix well until sugar is dissolved.
2. Mix in the rest of the ingredients. Stir and mix well.
3. Allow mixture to come to a low boil while stirring. Simmer for 5 to 7 minutes and remove from heat to cool. Store in a covered container in the refrigerator for up to 2 weeks.

Makes **2 CUPS (330 G)**

CURRY BOYS BBQ BRISKET RUB

A classic Texas brisket only needs two simple things: salt and pepper. As I'm sure you know by now, the flavor of the beef shines the most when you don't overcomplicate the rub. We use kosher salt and 16-mesh ground black pepper for the larger granules that give you a killer crunchy bark. Lastly, depending on the cook and what we want to pair with the brisket, we sometimes add white pepper to the rub for some earthier tones.

1 cup (102 g) ground black pepper (we prefer 16-mesh grind)
5 tablespoons (32 g) ground white pepper
½ cup + 3 tablespoons (198 g) kosher salt

1. Combine all ingredients and mix well.
2. Store in an airtight container and use as needed. Best within 2 months.

CURRY BOYS BBQ RUBS

As opposed to a wet brine or marinade, when using a dry rub on a cut of meat, we prefer to simply apply the rub just before smoking. While some pitmasters will season the day before, we find that salting too early can begin to cure the meat, subtly altering its texture and drawing out moisture before it's time to cook. So we prefer to season just before smoking to keep the surface moisture locked in and maintain a fresh, vibrant bark.

We like to apply the rubs using recycled seasoning shakers. Make sure to use one with large enough holes for all the larger granules, and always give the container a good swirl every few seconds, as the heavier components can separate from the lighter ones.

C.B. BRISKET RUB
C.B. PORK RUB
POULTRY RUB

Makes **2 CUPS (240 G)**

CURRY BOYS BBQ POULTRY RUB

For our poultry rub, we like to spice things up by adding Cajun seafood boil seasoning. It might seem odd, but seafood boil seasoning has incredible flavor and is loaded with umami, so it shouldn't be relegated solely to seafood.

7½ teaspoons (45 g) kosher salt
¾ cup (77 g) 16-mesh black pepper
¾ cup (72 g) Cajun seafood boil spice (such as Zatarain's Crab Boil or Slap Ya Mama)
3 tablespoons (27 g) granulated garlic
3 tablespoons (18 g) granulated chicken bouillon

1. Combine all ingredients and mix well.
2. Store in an airtight container and use as needed. Best within 2 months.

Makes **2 CUPS (320 G)**

CURRY BOYS BBQ PORK RUB

We think pork always tastes better when you introduce a little sweetness. The palm sugar brilliantly balances the Cajun seafood seasoning with hints of caramel and butterscotch.

¼ cup (72 g) kosher salt
½ cup (51 g) 16-mesh black pepper
½ cup (48 g) Cajun seafood boil spice (such as Zatarain's Crab Boil or Slap Ya Mama)
¼ cup (48 g) palm sugar or brown sugar
¼ cup (52 g) white sugar
¼ cup (36 g) granulated garlic

1. Combine all ingredients and mix well.
2. Store in an airtight container and use as needed. Best within 2 months.

Curry Boys Barbecue

Makes 2 CUPS (475 ML)

MAMA HO'S VIETNAMESE ALL-PURPOSE MEAT MARINADE

Andrew Ho's mother is a saint. I've known her since I was in high school, and she's always been a wizard in the kitchen. One of the things that she does really well when cooking is seasoning and marinating her proteins. This is really an unsung hero of cooking fundamentals, and she just has an inherent talent at infusing flavor. This marinade in particular is a versatile meat marinade that can be used for any sort of grilling and smoking. Classically, in Vietnamese culture, every family will likely have their own iteration of this marinade. But let's be real, Mama Ho's is the GOAT. —Sean

½ cup + 2 tablespoons (148 ml) lemon-lime soda (like Sprite)
5 tablespoons (95 g) oyster sauce
5 tablespoons (75 g) brown sugar
¼ cup (18 g) finely minced lemongrass
2 tablespoons (20 g) minced garlic
1½ tablespoons (22 ml) fish sauce
1½ tablespoons (23 ml) soy sauce
2 teaspoons paprika

1. In a large mixing bowl, combine soda, oyster sauce, and brown sugar. Mix well.
2. Add the rest of the ingredients and mix well.
3. Use as a marinade when grilling beef, chicken, or pork! For best results when grilling, we suggest marinating for 4-plus hours. For smoking, we recommend basting every 30 minutes at 225°F (107°C).

NOTE:
Use Nước Chấm (page 49) as a dipping sauce!

Makes **1 CUP (235 ML)**

THAI-INSPIRED LEMON PEPPER MARINADE

You can start calling yourself the Lemon Peppa Steppa after making this lemon pepper marinade. You get an incredibly zesty, slightly spicy, and peppery finish to anything you marinate! Smoked, or grilled, wings are an obvious choice, but this marinade will blow your mind with fried tofu or boiled shrimp.

¼ cup (60 ml) lemon juice
2 tablespoons (12 g) fresh lemon zest
1½ tablespoons (27 g) kosher salt
1½ tablespoons (10 g) ground black pepper
1½ tablespoons (18 g) palm sugar or brown sugar
1 tablespoon (9 g) lemongrass powder (sub with Thai curry powder if needed)

1. In a large mixing bowl, combine all ingredients and mix well.
2. Store in a covered container in the refrigerator for up to 1 week.

Makes ½ **CUP (120 ML)**

CRISPY GARLIC *CHILI OIL*

A good chili oil elevates everything it touches. Our chili oil is extremely garlicky, legitimately spicy, and perfectly savory. We literally put it on just about any dish—whether it's plain jasmine rice, delicious smoked brisket, or fragrant green curry. The ultimate combo breaker is pairing this chili oil with our tangy pickles. It's utter perfection, we think. Find the fried garlic in bags at your local Asian market.

½ cup (120 ml) vegetable oil
1½ tablespoons (5 g) Thai chili flakes or powder
1½ tablespoons (5 g) crushed red pepper flakes
⅔ teaspoon salt
¼ cup (38 g) fried garlic

1. In a small saucepan, add vegetable oil, Thai chili, and crushed red pepper flakes. Turn to low to medium heat.
2. Add in salt once oil begins to bubble a little bit, while constantly stirring. Add in fried garlic and turn off heat.
3. Let mixture cool. Store in a covered container in the refrigerator for up to 1 month.

Makes **1 CUP (235 ML)**

HONEY *SRIRACHA* SAUCE

With the hot honey craze sweeping across the country, this super simple sauce is the Asian-inspired equivalent. It's got insane depth from the sriracha (we prefer Huy Fong) and an almost lacquerlike finish because of the honey. It goes so well with anything fried, grilled, or smoked. If you want to punch up the heat a little bit more, just add more sriracha than the recipe dictates. It goes great with BBQ shrimp, grilled chicken, or over pulled pork sandwiches!

½ cup (170 g) honey
½ cup (120 g) sriracha
¼ cup (60 ml) warm water, divided

1. In a medium mixing bowl, whisk together honey and sriracha. Slowly add 1 tablespoon (15 ml) of warm water into the sauce mixture while mixing. Continue adding water until all is combined and the sauce is a liquid consistency.

Pictured clockwise from top left: Thai Sriracha Buffalo Sauce (page 48), Nước Chấm (Classic Vietnamese Dipping Sauce) (page 49), Honey Sriracha Sauce (this page)

Makes 1¼ CUPS (285 ML)

THAI SRIRACHA BUFFALO SAUCE

Classic buffalo sauce often feels too "one-note." Very few places make it balanced well, and typically it is either too hot sauce–forward or too vinegar-forward. Our buffalo sauce adds little hints of sweetness and earthiness that create a sauce that is silky and spicy like classic buffalo, but is also not too sour or too spicy. This is one of our go-to sauces when we are grilling or smoking chicken or seafood that we know our friends and family will love. This recipe can sauce 4 to 5 pounds (1.8 to 2.3 kg) of chicken wings (40 to 50 wings). We highly recommend pairing this sauce with an ice-cold Chang or Singha beer.

½ cup (112 g) unsalted butter
¼ cup (60 ml) fish sauce
3½ tablespoons (53 g) sriracha
2 tablespoons (24 g) palm sugar or brown sugar
2 tablespoons (30 ml) lime juice
2 tablespoons (30 ml) rice vinegar
1 tablespoon (15 ml) soy sauce
2 cloves garlic, minced
½ teaspoon white pepper
½ teaspoon Thai chili flakes
1 teaspoon grated ginger or to taste

1. In a small or medium saucepan, slowly melt unsalted butter on low to medium heat. Once butter has melted, add in everything but the ginger. Combine and mix well.
2. Turn heat to low and simmer sauce for 4 to 5 minutes until everything is combined well. Make sure heat is low enough so that you don't burn the garlic!
3. Add in ginger and stir on low heat. Simmer for 2 minutes, allowing sauce to thicken slightly. Remove sauce from heat and allow it to cool down a little.
4. When sauce has cooled but is still warm, toss with chicken wings or use as a baste on the smoker or grill! Store in a covered container in the refrigerator for up to 1 week.

PRO TIP:
Garnish with chopped Thai basil, and people will love you forever!

Makes **1¼ CUPS (285 ML)**

NƯỚC CHẤM *(CLASSIC VIETNAMESE DIPPING SAUCE)*

This might be the pound-for-pound champ when it comes to popular Southeast Asian sauces. It is Vietnamese in origin, but it goes with just about anything: proteins, vegetables, rice, noodles, you name it. Every little Asian kid has a story about it, and every Asian adult has a healthy obsession with it. It works so well because it combines umami, sweetness, tanginess, and spice all in one cohesive blend. Although there are several variations, our version is pretty standard, and as the recipe dictates, you should always have a little jar in the fridge to level up any dish.

½ cup (118 ml) fish sauce
¼ cup (60 ml) lime juice
¼ cup (52 g) white sugar
½ cup (118 ml) water
2 cloves garlic, minced or sliced
4 Thai chilies, finely sliced

1. In a medium mixing bowl, mix all ingredients together until sugar is dissolved. Use with smoked or grilled proteins, or lightly as a salad dressing! We always have a jar of this in our fridge ready to go.

PRO TIP:

Although the refrigerated shelf life is around a week, we highly recommend using the sauce within 2 to 3 days. The initial brightness of the sauce begins to dull and mellow the longer it sits!

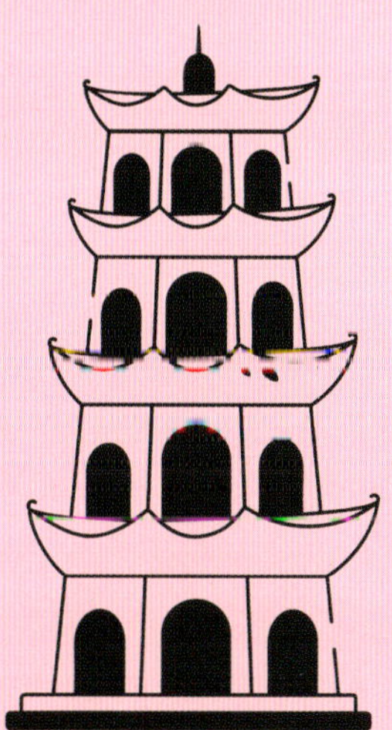

Makes 1 CUP (235 ML)

PRIK NAM PLA (SALTY and SPICY THAI DIPPING SAUCE)

Thai people love *their sauces—and for good reason. You'll find sauce caddies at every street food establishment and restaurant in Thailand with their own versions of classic sauces and spices to complement the food they're serving. One of the fundamental differences between Thai cooking and, say, French cooking, is that in Thailand, many chefs and cooks welcome the guest to adjust the dish to their liking, whether it is via adding spice or a sauce. Prik nam pla may just be the greatest sauce of them all. It's certainly the most popular and has become synonymous with authentic Thai cuisine. This versatile sauce is perfectly salty, sour, and spicy, and goes well with just about anything, though it goes great with fatty smoked meats like pork belly and brisket burnt ends. A must for salty, spicy, and umami lovers!*

2 tablespoons (18 g) thinly sliced Thai red chili
6 tablespoons (89 ml) fish sauce
2½ tablespoons (37 ml) lime juice
4 cloves garlic, minced
3 tablespoons (30 g) finely sliced shallots

1. In a medium mixing bowl, mix together all ingredients. Combine and mix well. Store in a covered container in the refrigerator for up to 1 week.

Pictured clockwise from top right: Prik Nam Pla (Salty and Spicy Thai Dipping Sauce) (this page), Jeow Som (Lao-Style Dipping Sauce) (page 53), Nam Jim Jaew (Thai Spicy and Tangy Dipping Sauce) (page 52)

Makes **1 CUP (235 ML)**

NAM JIM JAEW (THAI SPICY *and* TANGY DIPPING SAUCE)

Nam jim jaew is an extremely versatile sauce that goes absolutely perfectly with grilled and smoked meats because of the citrus, spice, and funk. The sauce is super easy to make, and the toasted rice powder is what sets it apart from similar sauces like the jeow som. The toasted rice adds a little bit of texture and a unique, smoky aroma. Originally from the Isaan region of Northeast Thailand, it has since proliferated throughout all of Thailand due to how delicious it is!

- 3½ tablespoons (35 g) uncooked jasmine rice
- 3 tablespoons (45 g) tamarind paste
- ¼ cup (60 ml) lime juice
- ¼ cup (60 ml) fish sauce
- 2 teaspoons palm sugar or brown sugar
- 2 teaspoons Thai chili flakes (adjust to spiciness preference)
- 2 tablespoons (6 g) finely chopped green onions
- 2 tablespoons (20 g) diced shallots
- 2 tablespoons (2 g) finely chopped cilantro

1. Make the toasted rice powder: Heat a medium-sized dry pan to low to medium heat. Add uncooked jasmine rice to pan and toss and toast until golden brown, 3 to 5 minutes. Remove from heat and cool, then grind toasted rice into a powder using a spice grinder or mortar and pestle. You should have about 2 tablespoons of toasted rice powder.
2. In a medium mixing bowl, add tamarind paste, lime juice, fish sauce, and sugar. Combine and mix well until sugar is dissolved.
3. Add in chili flakes, green onions, toasted rice powder, shallots, and cilantro. Mix well, making sure everything is combined. It goes fantastically with smoked and grilled beef and pork dishes—a personal favorite of Andrew Ho! Store in a covered container in the refrigerator for up to 1 week.

Makes 1 CUP (235 ML)

JEOW SOM
(LAO-STYLE DIPPING SAUCE)

Jeow som is our favorite sauce, and it is a runaway favorite at Curry Boys BBQ when we serve it with our pork ribs. Andrew Ho will use this with absolutely everything (I've even seen him dip plain ol' tortillas in the sauce as a snack). It goes particularly well with smoked or grilled proteins—particularly with beef or pork. A little goes a long way, and you can certainly adjust the spice level in this sauce to your liking. What this sauce does really well is complement the protein without completely covering up its natural richness and flavor. It's the antithesis of classic steak sauce. In fact, this is one of those sauces that I wish would become a staple at steak houses all over the United States. —Sean

¼ cup + 1 tablespoon (74 ml) lime juice
3½ tablespoons (52 ml) fish sauce, plus more to taste
3 tablespoons (30 g) finely minced shallots
2 tablespoons (2 g) finely minced cilantro
1½ tablespoons (18 g) palm sugar or brown sugar, plus more to taste
1 tablespoon (9 g) finely sliced Thai chili (adjust to spiciness preference)
1 teaspoon thinly sliced clove garlic

1. In a medium mixing bowl, mix together all ingredients. Mix well until sugar is dissolved.
2. Taste and add a touch of fish sauce or sugar as needed. You are looking for a balanced overall taste. Serve with grilled or smoked beef. Store in a covered container in the refrigerator for up to 1 week.

chapter
2

APPETIZERS AND SMALL PLATES

CURRY QUESO

This silky, thick queso is made extra creamy and rich with a hint of Penang curry. It goes so well with sausage or pulled pork, or you could just dip in some tortilla chips for a simple starter. It's a genetic travesty that I'm lactose intolerant, but I'm willing to risk it for this queso. —Sean

¾ pound (340 g) white American cheese
¾ cup (177 ml) water
½ cup (118 ml) 2 percent milk
1 teaspoon Thai Penang curry paste
⅛ teaspoon granulated garlic
⅛ teaspoon granulated onion
⅛ teaspoon Cajun seasoning
⅛ teaspoon chicken bouillon powder

1. In a small or medium saucepan, turn heat to low and add cheese, water, and milk. Stir until cheese is fully melted, then mix in the remaining ingredients.
2. Serve hot with your favorite tortilla chips, over hot dogs, or poured over our famous Curry Boys BBQ Pulled Pork Nachos (page 60)! Store in a covered container in the refrigerator for up to 1 week.

Serves **4**

GREEN CURRY GUACAMOLE

Look, no hate to traditional guacamole. In fact, I love guacamole, but this green curry guacamole is so uniquely delicious that it makes me angry it isn't more accessible. So, here's the deal: We need you to make this guacamole all the time for your cool, hip friends so that this recipe can get the national exposure that it deserves. The guacamole is tangy, nutty, and floral, making this the perfect dip for salty chips or crisps. We love dipping shrimp chips or wonton chips to keep things nice and Asian-inspired, but tortilla chips are just as perfect. Also, I said the word "guacamole" six times. Is that too many times? —Sean

3 ripe avocados
1 teaspoon Thai green curry paste
1 tablespoon (15 ml) lime juice, plus more as needed
1 tablespoon (1 g) chopped cilantro, plus more as needed
½ red onion, finely diced
½ small Roma tomato, diced
½ teaspoon smoked paprika
½ teaspoon salt, plus more as needed
½ jalapeño, finely diced
1 clove garlic, minced
1 tablespoon (9 g) crushed or chopped roasted peanuts

1. In a medium mixing bowl, mash avocados until they are smooth, but leave some small pieces of avocado for texture.
2. In a separate small mixing bowl, mix green curry paste with lime juice until fully combined.
3. Stir this curry mixture into the mashed avocados, making sure everything is mixed well. Add in cilantro, red onion, tomato, paprika, salt, jalapeño, and garlic. If needed, add more lime juice or salt to taste. Garnish with crushed peanuts and chopped cilantro. Serve with your favorite tortilla chips or shrimp chips!

Serves **4**

CURRY BOYS
BBQ PULLED PORK NACHOS

We think nachos are unfairly categorized as only being an appetizer, but with these pulled pork nachos, you're probably not going to want to share them anyway! The pulled pork is incredibly juicy to the point where you'll likely need a formidable napkin or an extra-absorbent paper towel, and the combination of sweet honey sriracha, bold curry queso, and crispy tortilla chips is like the BBQ version of sex, drugs, and rock and roll. This is one of our best sellers in the restaurant. It's perfect for parties and an absolute crowd favorite in San Antonio and Nashville!

12 ounces (340 g) tortilla chips
1 quart (946 ml) Curry Queso (page 56), divided
4 ounces (120 g) Honey Sriracha Sauce (page 46), divided
1 pound (454 g) hot, chopped Smoked and Pulled Pork (page 187)
¼ cup (4 g) chopped cilantro

1. For each serving, lay a bed of tortilla chips to cover a medium serving platter.
2. Ladle ½ cup (120 ml) of queso evenly onto the chips. Then, evenly add about 2 tablespoons (28 ml) of honey sriracha over queso and chips.
3. Add 4 ounces of pulled pork evenly onto the chips, making sure everything looks presentable.
4. Ladle another ½ cup (120 ml) of queso evenly onto the pulled pork. Follow with another 2 tablespoons (28 ml) of honey sriracha over everything. Garnish nachos with chopped cilantro.

Serves **4 TO 6**

SMOKED *and* STEAMED CHICKEN *and* SHRIMP DUMPLINGS

Dumplings are probably the reason why I'm here today. Like many other Chinese children, when I was younger, my assistance was always requested by my beautiful mother when she was making dumplings. As a child, I always loved it because it reminded me of edible modeling clay. As I got older, my mom didn't have to ask me to help because I started to just genuinely enjoy being in the kitchen with her. This was the start of my dream. Dumplings planted the seed, and I am so grateful to have a mother who wanted to spend that time with me. This recipe is a unique take on the traditional Chinese dumpling that uses smoked shrimp and chicken to get a velvety texture and a subtle smoky aroma.

My mom would use store-bought dumpling wrappers because she always said that they tasted just as good and required half the labor. So, for this recipe, we recommend going to your local Asian market. Look for Dynasty, Twin Marquis, or Twin Dragon brands; as long as the wrapper isn't too thick, and is specifically made for dumplings, then you should be good to go! —Sean

For the filling:

½ pound (227 g) shrimp, minced (with knife or food processor)
½ pound (227 g) ground chicken
3 tablespoons (9 g) minced green onions
1½ tablespoons (1.5 g) minced cilantro
½ tablespoon grated ginger
1 clove garlic, minced
1 tablespoon (19 g) oyster sauce
1 tablespoon (15 ml) light soy sauce
1 teaspoon white sugar
½ tablespoon sesame oil
½ tablespoon rice vinegar
1 tablespoon (8 g) cornstarch
16 dumpling wrappers

Ingredients continued

1. Make the marinade: Preheat smoker to 225°F (107°C). Line a sheet tray with parchment paper or foil. In a large mixing bowl, combine and mix all dumpling filling ingredients. Mix well to ensure everything is evenly combined. Spread out dumpling filling on the tray and smoke for 45 minutes or until filling reaches an internal temperature of 165°F (74°C). Remove from smoker and let cool for 15 to 20 minutes. Using clean hands or wearing gloves, break apart dumpling filling into small, ground meat–like pieces.
2. Lay out 16 dumpling wrappers and place 1 tablespoon (14 g) of filling onto the center of each wrapper. Using clean fingers, moisten the edge of the wrapper with warm water and then fold the wrapper to close and cover the filling. Repeat for all dumplings.
3. Line a steam basket with parchment paper to keep the dumplings from sticking. Place the dumplings into the basket. Set the steamer basket over a pot of boiling water and steam for 8 to 10 minutes (check dumpling wrapper instructions!) until the wrappers are slightly translucent and dumplings are piping hot.

Continued

For the sauce:

- 2 tablespoons Crispy Garlic Chili Oil (page 45)
- 2 tablespoons (30 ml) light soy sauce
- 2 teaspoons sugar
- 1 tablespoon (15 ml) rice vinegar
- 2 teaspoons sesame oil
- 1 teaspoon sesame seeds, for garnish
- 1 teaspoon green onions, sliced finely, for garnish

4. Make the sauce: In a medium mixing bowl, mix all dumpling sauce ingredients together.
5. Serve dumplings piping hot, garnished with green onions and sesame seeds, on a large serving platter with sides of dumpling sauce!

Serves **6**

THAI STREET-STYLE SMOKED *and* GRILLED CHICKEN SATAY SKEWERS *with* PEANUT SAUCE

This is one of our favorite snacks to eat anytime we visit a Thai restaurant in North America. The really great Thai joints will have a perfectly marinated and charred piece of juicy chicken thigh with a savory and not overly sweet peanut sauce. It's unctuous, approachable, and undeniably delicious. Interestingly, if you're in Thailand gallivanting around, you may actually struggle to find chicken satay skewers—unless you are in a tourist zone or in an area with a large Muslim community. Because pork is king in Thailand, pork satay is much easier to find and the most popular version of this street food.

For the marinade:

1½ cups (336 g) coconut milk
3 tablespoons (45 ml) soy sauce
3 tablespoons (45 ml) fish sauce
3 tablespoons (36 g) palm sugar or brown sugar
2 tablespoons (12 g) Thai red curry powder (sub 1 tablespoon [15 g] Thai red curry paste)
1 tablespoon (7 g) turmeric powder
1 tablespoon (6 g) ginger
1 tablespoon (10 g) garlic, minced
1 tablespoon (5 g) lemongrass, minced finely
1 teaspoon white pepper

3 pounds (1.4 kg) boneless, skinless chicken thigh, cut into 1-inch (2.5 cm) strips

Ingredients continued

1. Make the marinade: In a large mixing bowl, combine marinade ingredients. Add in the raw chicken strips and mix, making sure the meat is coated evenly. Marinate in the refrigerator for at least 2 hours, or overnight for the best flavor!

Continued

Continued from previous page

For the peanut sauce:

1 cup (224 g) coconut milk
½ cup (130 g) creamy peanut butter
2 tablespoons (30 ml) soy sauce
2 tablespoons (24 g) palm sugar or brown sugar
1 tablespoon (15 g) Thai red curry paste
2 tablespoons (30 ml) fish sauce
1 tablespoon (15 ml) fresh lime juice
½ teaspoon Thai chili powder or flakes (adjust to spiciness preference)

For the pickles:

1 small cucumber, sliced into half moons
1 shallot, sliced
2 Thai chilies, sliced (adjust to spiciness preference)
½ cup (118 ml) white vinegar
¼ cup (50 g) white sugar
½ teaspoon salt
¼ cup (60 ml) water

Red onion, sliced
Cucumber, sliced
Lime wedges

2. Make the peanut sauce: In a small saucepan, combine all sauce ingredients. Simmer sauce on low heat, stirring to make sure it doesn't burn and is mixed well. Sauce should be smooth and reduced.
3. Make the pickles: Set aside cucumber, shallots, and Thai chilies in a medium-sized jar. In a medium saucepan over medium heat, combine vinegar, sugar, salt, and water until sugar and salt are dissolved. Be careful not to bring to a boil; we just want everything to be dissolved. Remove from heat and set aside to cool. Add cooled pickling liquid to the jar. Ensure the vegetables are fully submerged in the pickling liquid. Let sit in the jar at room temperature for at least 1 hour for best results.
4. Preheat smoker to 225°F (107°C). If using bamboo skewers, soak in water so they don't burn. You can use metal skewers if you have them. Put marinated chicken strips onto the smoker grates and smoke for 45 to 60 minutes until chicken is cooked to 165°F (74°C). Reserve leftover marinade.
5. Preheat grill to medium to high heat. Skewer smoked chicken strips and grill chicken for about 2 minutes per side, basting chicken with extra meat marinade until skewers look charred to your liking.
6. Place skewers neatly in a row on a large serving platter. Serve with pickles, peanut sauce, red onion, cucumber, and lime wedges. Enjoy with jasmine rice if you want to eat this as a full meal!

GRILLED *THAI SRIRACHA* BUFFALO WINGS

While we all know by now that Andrew Samia is a big "wing guy," I much prefer grilled wings. It isn't because I'm some health nut, but I usually prefer a charred flavor over a fried, oily flavor. Grilling allows for nuance and complexity—as some parts are charred and slightly bitter, and other spots are fatty and juicy. When you pair grilled wings with our Thai Sriracha Buffalo Sauce, this dish is a no-brainer. It's perfect while watching your favorite sports team (hopefully) beat their bitter rivals, but at least you've got these wings to fall back on if they lose. —Sean

4 pounds (1.8 kg) chicken wings, flats and drumette pieces separated
1½ tablespoons (22 ml) vegetable oil
1 teaspoon salt
½ teaspoon black pepper
1¼ cups (285 ml) Thai Sriracha Buffalo Sauce (page 48)
1 teaspoon sesame seeds
3 tablespoons (3 g) chopped cilantro
2 tablespoons (5 g) chopped Thai basil
2 tablespoons (7 g) sliced Thai chili
8 lime wedges

1. Preheat grill to medium to high heat. In a large mixing bowl, combine and mix chicken wings, vegetable oil, salt, and black pepper.
2. Place wings on grill grates, making sure they are not touching. Grill for 13 to 15 minutes, flipping wings halfway through to prevent any burning. After 13 to 15 minutes, begin to baste wings with sauce. Flip wings every 5 minutes while continuing to baste with sauce. Wings should be finished after 3 or 4 basting cycles, when they have a nice char or caramelization.
3. Neatly plate wings on a large serving platter in rows. Garnish wings with sesame seeds, cilantro, Thai basil, Thai chilies, and lime!

Pictured clockwise from top left: Smoked and Fried Thai Red Curry Lemon Pepper Wings (page 70), Fish Sauce–Caramel Smoked Wings (page 71), Grilled Thai Sriracha Buffalo Wings (this page)

SMOKED *and* FRIED THAI RED CURRY *LEMON PEPPER WINGS*

Wings are Andrew Samia's guilty pleasure, and it doesn't have to be the Super Bowl or a massive sporting event to have them. He eats them on school nights, weekends, National Tax Day, Halloween, dinner parties, and Quinceañeras. Smoking the wings tenderizes and imparts a layer of barbecued depth, and frying them gives you that crispy skin we all crave. While lemon pepper is the flavor we prefer, this wing marinade goes well with most savory rubs and spices. Lemongrass powder can be found at Asian markets, but you can substitute Thai curry powder if need be.

For the marinade:

¼ cup (60 ml) soy sauce
2 tablespoons (30 ml) fish sauce
1 tablespoon (15 ml) lime juice
1 tablespoon (15 ml) rice vinegar
1 tablespoon (12 g) palm sugar or brown sugar
1 tablespoon (6 g) Thai red curry powder
2 cloves garlic, minced
1 teaspoon grated ginger
1 teaspoon turmeric powder
½ teaspoon black pepper
½ teaspoon chili flakes or powder (adjust to spiciness preference)

16 whole chicken wings
2 tablespoons (30 ml) vegetable oil to coat wings
Vegetable oil for frying

For the seasoning:

2 tablespoons (30 ml) lemon juice
2 teaspoons fresh lemon zest
1 teaspoon salt
1 teaspoon 16-mesh black pepper
1 teaspoon palm sugar or white sugar
1 teaspoon (9 g) lemongrass powder (sub Thai curry powder)

Thai chilies, sliced
¼ cup (4 g) chopped cilantro
Lime wedges

1. Make the marinade: In a large mixing bowl, combine marinade ingredients. Add in chicken wings and mix well, making sure meat is coated evenly. Cover bowl and let marinate in the refrigerator for 1 hour or overnight for the best flavor!
2. Preheat smoker to 225°F (107°C). Toss marinated wings with 2 tablespoons (30 ml) oil, then put on smoker grate and make sure they are evenly spaced out. Smoke wings for 1½ to 2 hours until they reach internal temperature of 155°F (68°C).
3. Heat up 3 inches (7.6 cm) of vegetable oil in a large pot or fryer to 350°F (180°C). Slowly and carefully drop the smoked wings into the oil, frying wings in small batches. Fry for about 4 to 5 minutes until wings are crispy and golden in color and reach an internal temperature of 165°F (74°C). Remove from oil and drain on paper towels on a plate.
4. Make the seasoning: In a large mixing bowl, combine seasoning ingredients thoroughly.
5. Once all wings are fried, toss them in lemon pepper seasoning immediately, making sure the meat is coated evenly.
6. Place wings neatly on a large serving platter. Garnish with sliced Thai chilies and chopped cilantro, and serve with lime wedges on the side.

Serves 8

FISH SAUCE–CARAMEL SMOKED WINGS

Fish sauce–caramel wings are one of the most iconic Vietnamese appetizers and hold a special place in my heart. I remember being (slightly) inebriated one late night in 2015, wandering around the streets of Ho Chi Minh City with Andrew Ho, looking for a late-night snack. We eventually stumbled upon a spot serving some fish sauce–caramel fried wings that smelled so good, I thought I was in heaven. Ho and I sat on some tiny plastic stools, and as we devoured these wings—burning the roofs of our mouths in the process—we dreamed up an idea to open our first restaurant. We look back so fondly at this memory and wanted to re-create a version of this dish to honor this moment in our lives. Our version is smoked first—to pay homage to Andrew Samia, who helped make our dream become a reality—and then broiled and tossed in a sweet and funky sauce for a crispy, umami bomb of a bite. —Sean

4 pounds (1.8 kg) chicken wings, flats and drumette pieces separated
1 tablespoon (18 g) kosher salt
1 teaspoon garlic powder
1 teaspoon black pepper
½ teaspoon white pepper
1 tablespoon (15 ml) vegetable oil
1 tablespoon (8 g) cornstarch

Ingredients continued

1. Preheat smoker to 225°F (107°C). Preheat oven to low broiler setting. Cover a sheet pan with parchment paper. Make sure wings are dry, or with minimal moisture. Paper towels work well. Add them to a large mixing bowl.
2. In a small mixing bowl, mix salt, garlic powder, black pepper, white pepper, and vegetable oil. Add in chicken wings and mix well, making sure wings are evenly coated. Dust wings lightly with the cornstarch and mix in the bowl again.
3. Place wings on smoker grates, making sure they are not touching. Smoke for 1½ to 2 hours or until internal temperature reaches 165°F to 170°F (74°C to 77°C). Remove wings and place them on the sheet pan with parchment paper, making sure they are not touching. Broil on low in oven for 7 to 8 minutes, flipping halfway through to make sure wings are evenly crisped.

Continued from previous page

For the sauce:

¼ cup (60 ml) fish sauce
¼ cup (60 g) brown sugar
2 tablespoons (40 g) honey
2 tablespoons (30 ml) rice vinegar
1 tablespoon (15 ml) soy sauce
3 cloves garlic, minced
1 Thai chili, sliced (adjust to spiciness preference)
½ teaspoon white pepper
1 tablespoon (15 ml) fresh lime juice

¼ cup (35 g) crushed roasted peanuts
2 tablespoons (6 g) chopped green onions
2 tablespoons (2 g) chopped cilantro
1 tablespoon (4 g) sliced Thai chilies
8 lime wedges

4. Make the sauce: Meanwhile, in a medium saucepan on low to medium heat, combine all sauce ingredients except lime juice. Combine well on a low simmer for 4 to 5 minutes, until sauce begins to slightly thicken. Remove from heat and slowly stir in lime juice. Set aside.
5. Transfer wings from sheet pan to a clean large mixing bowl. Drizzle the sauce over the wings while tossing. Make sure the wings are evenly coated. Plate wings neatly on a large serving platter. Garnish with crushed peanuts, green onions, cilantro, Thai chilies, and lime wedges.

Makes **12 BAO BUNS, TO SERVE 4 TO 6 AS AN APPETIZER**

CRYING TIGER
SMOKED BRISKET BAO BUNS

When Andrew Ho first returned to the United States in 2016—fresh off a three-year stint in Thailand and Vietnam—he craved Thai food and Thai flavors so badly. We were living in San Antonio and admittedly, there just aren't too many Asian restaurants in the city—let alone Thai restaurants that could hold a candle to a Thai auntie at a Bangkok night market. I had heard of a new Thai restaurant that opened nearby, so I called Andrew Samia to meet us there. We ordered the Tiger Cry Salad as a starter and upon the first bite, I nearly saw Ho's eyes pop out of his head. It was so unfathomably good. Shout-out to Baan Isaan: You were ahead of your time and weren't appreciated enough. Samia always said he wished he could eat this dish in a sandwich-form, so our recipe incorporates a pillowy Chinese bao bun into the citrusy, tangy, and fatty mix. The bao bun's sweetness offsets the brisket's richness and allows you to inhale a couple of these at a time without feeling too full! —Sean

2 pounds (907 g) Texas-Style Smoked Beef Brisket (can use leftovers), chopped until shredded (page 157)

2 tablespoons (30 ml) beef broth, optional

For the crying tiger sauce:

3 tablespoons (45 ml) fish sauce

2 tablespoons (30 ml) lime juice

1 tablespoon (15 g) tamarind paste

1 tablespoon (12 g) palm sugar or brown sugar

1 tablespoon (5 g) toasted rice powder (page 52)

1 tablespoon (3 g) chopped green onions

1 tablespoon (1 g) chopped cilantro

½ teaspoon Thai chili flakes (adjust to spiciness preference)

1 clove garlic, minced

½ teaspoon black pepper

Ingredients continued

1. If using cold brisket, chop and reheat in a large pan over medium heat with beef broth for moisture. Remove the pan from heat and set to the side. If using freshly cooked brisket, slice and chop until brisket is shredded.
2. Make the crying tiger sauce: In a large mixing bowl, mix together all the sauce ingredients. Toss hot brisket into the sauce and gently mix well, make sure everything is coated evenly.

Continued

For the mayo:

½ cup (115 g) mayonnaise (we prefer Duke's)
1 tablespoon (15 g) tamarind paste
1 teaspoon honey
1 teaspoon sriracha
1 teaspoon lime juice
½ teaspoon garlic powder
Pinch salt, to taste
Pinch black pepper, to taste

For the slaw:

1 cup (70 g) shredded green cabbage
½ cup (55 g) shredded carrots
¼ cup (40 g) thinly sliced red onion
¼ cup (10 g) chopped Thai basil
¼ cup (4 g) chopped cilantro
1 Thai chili, sliced thinly
1 tablespoon (15 ml) fish sauce
2 tablespoons (30 ml) lime juice
1 teaspoon white sugar

12 steamed bao buns (can be found at Asian market)
½ cup (8 g) chopped cilantro

3. Make the mayo: In a medium mixing bowl, whisk together the mayo ingredients. Cover and refrigerate until ready to serve.
4. Make the slaw: In a large mixing bowl, combine and mix all the vegetables and herbs. In a separate small mixing bowl, combine and mix the fish sauce, lime juice, and sugar. Drizzle the dressing over the vegetable mixture while tossing. Make sure everything is evenly coated. Cover and refrigerate until ready to serve
5. Steam the bao buns according to package directions. Spread a healthy amount of the mayo onto the top inside flap of each bao bun. Add a healthy amount of crying tiger brisket on the bottom side of the bao bun. Top brisket with herb slaw and garnish with chopped cilantro. Serve bao buns neatly in rows on a large serving platter!

Makes 12 POPPERS, SERVES 4 TO 6

RED CURRY BRISKET-STUFFED JALAPEÑO POPPERS

Jalapeño poppers are a big deal in Texas—particularly during a backyard BBQ or a big game. They're essentially a mini chili relleno, but with an indulgent, one-bite appeal! The mix of curry paste and cream cheese brings the silky balance of savory and sweet, and the smoked brisket adds richness. You might want to consider making a double batch of these, because our friend ate six of them in one sitting when we were testing this recipe out. He kept claiming he was "verifying the consistency."

4 ounces (113 g) cream cheese, softened
½ cup (113 g) chopped Texas-Style Smoked Beef Brisket (can use leftovers) (page 157)
½ cup (58 g) shredded sharp cheddar cheese
1 green onion, sliced finely
1 teaspoon Thai red curry paste
1 teaspoon lime juice
Pinch salt
Pinch black pepper
6 large jalapeños, halved lengthwise, seeds and insides removed
3 tablespoons (60 g) Honey Sriracha Sauce (optional, page 46)
¼ cup (4 g) chopped cilantro

1. In a medium mixing bowl, combine cream cheese, smoked brisket, cheddar cheese, green onion, red curry paste, lime juice, salt, and pepper. Mix well to make sure everything is evenly combined.
2. Place the 12 jalapeño halves, open face up, on a parchment paper–lined baking sheet. Using a tablespoon, scoop brisket and cream cheese mixture into each jalapeño. Do not overfill. Use bottom of spoon to press on top of brisket mixture to flatten.
3. Preheat smoker to 275°F (135°C). Place the tray of poppers onto smoker grates. Smoke for 35 to 40 minutes until the cream cheese and cheddar cheese are melted and the jalapeños look like they have absorbed some smoke. Remove from smoker and serve hot on an appetizer platter drizzled with honey sriracha sauce, if using, and chopped cilantro!

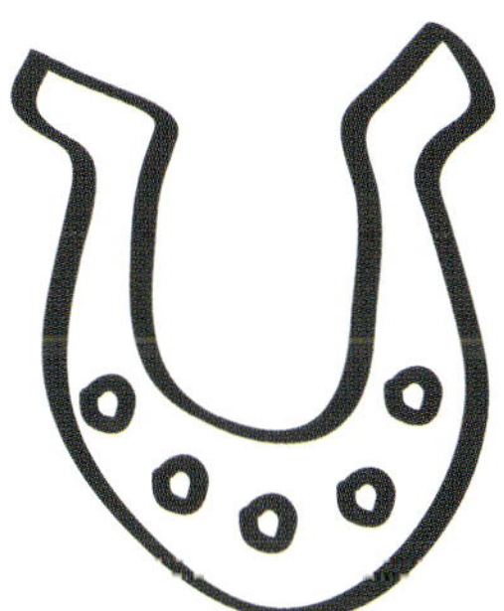

Makes **8 MEDIUM SPRING ROLLS**

FRESH PULLED PORK SPRING ROLLS *with* PEANUT SAUCE

There are a couple things in life that we all know as inevitable: death, taxes, and Thanos. But we think it is time we add "ordering fresh spring rolls at a Vietnamese restaurant" to that list too. How can something be so fresh, yet so indulgent? Behold, the awesome power of fresh spring rolls. We add smoky pulled pork into the mix, but the real X factor is the peanut dipping sauce. It isn't too sweet, and it binds to the spring rolls perfectly—covering every nook and cranny of the rice paper. Eat two, or all eight of them. No one is judging you here.

For the peanut dipping sauce:

½ cup (125 g) hoisin sauce
¼ cup (65 g) creamy peanut butter
3½ tablespoons (52 ml) water
1 tablespoon (15 ml) rice vinegar
1 teaspoon sesame oil
1 clove garlic, minced
¼ cup (35 g) crushed roasted peanuts
2 tablespoons (30 g) sriracha

8 rice paper wrappers (9-inch-plus [23 cm] in diameter works best)
1 cup (200 g) cooked vermicelli noodles
1 cup (70 g) shredded lettuce (sub cabbage)
1 cup (110 g) julienned or shredded carrots
1 cucumber, cut into 6-inch (15 cm) slices
1 pound (454 g) hot Smoked and Pulled Pork (page 187)
½ cup (8 g) chopped cilantro
¼ cup (10 g) chopped Thai basil
¼ cup (24 g) chopped mint
Sriracha or sliced Thai chilies for garnish

1. Make the peanut dipping sauce: In a small saucepan on low heat, combine all sauce ingredients except peanuts and sriracha. Mix until smooth and ingredients are combined well, about 6 to 8 minutes. Stir in crushed peanuts and sriracha.
2. Make sure all of your spring roll ingredients are in their own bowls and ready to be assembled. Fill a large mixing bowl with warm water. Slowly dip a rice paper into the water, slowly coating with water, but not too much. Put the wet rice paper on a cutting board or flat surface. On one side of the rice paper, add noodles, lettuce, carrots, cucumber, pulled pork, cilantro, basil, and mint. Pull the shorter side of the rice paper over the top of the ingredients like a burrito and roll it. Tuck in the sides and continue rolling until spring roll is enclosed and tight. Repeat to make all the spring rolls.
3. Plate spring rolls neatly on a large serving platter. Serve with a side of peanut sauce and extra sriracha or Thai chilies!

Serves **4 TO 6**

VIETNAMESE-STYLE SCALLION OIL CHARGRILLED OYSTERS

Chargrilled oysters are an extremely popular street food in Vietnam. They're commonly eaten as a late-night snack with Saigon beer and other libations of the sort, but we include them with the appetizers here. Being inebriated might add to the experience, but trust us when we say that these oysters sing on their own. The combination of using scallion oil—a popular Vietnamese way to grill—and roasted peanuts creates the most unbelievable smell. If you were in Vietnam, we can promise that you'd pull your moped scooter over to order a half-dozen of these oysters. The good news is that you don't have to travel to Vietnam to experience this. And you also won't need to eat it while sitting on a comically small plastic stool.

For the green onion oil:

¼ cup (60 ml) vegetable oil
2 cloves garlic, minced
1 cup (48 g) finely chopped green onions
2 tablespoons (30 ml) fish sauce
1 tablespoon (13 g) white sugar

24 fresh cleaned and shucked oysters on the half shell
¼ cup (40 g) fried shallots
½ cup (75 g) crushed roasted peanuts
¼ cup (70 g) sambal chili garlic sauce
12 lime wedges
2 loaves French baguette, sliced and toasted

1. Make the green onion oil: In a small saucepan, heat vegetable oil on medium heat. Add garlic and sauté for 30 seconds (make sure not to burn!). Mix in green onions and cook for 30 seconds until they just become soft. Mix in fish sauce and white sugar until combined. Remove from pan and set aside in a bowl.
2. Heat a charcoal or propane grill to high heat. Put shucked oysters on the grill grates.
3. Add 1 teaspoon of the prepared green onion oil, with garlic and green onion bits, onto each oyster. Cover the grill for 3 to 4 minutes. Oysters are ready when they are bubbling and a bit firm!
4. Using tongs, carefully remove oysters from the grill and onto a large serving plate. Immediately garnish each oyster with a pinch of fried shallots and crushed peanuts. Serve oysters with sambal chili garlic sauce, lime wedges on the side, and a toasted French baguette to dip in the green onion oil and juices!

chapter
3

SMOKY SALADS AND SOUPS

CURRY BOYS BBQ

Serves 4

THAI-INSPIRED CUCUMBER SALAD

Fear not, carnivores; salads can be sexy too. This one in particular is the perfect complement to any meat-forward dinner party or meal. Take a bite of protein. Take a bite of this refreshing cucumber salad. Repeat until the meal is over or until you're perfectly satiated—which you will be, if you balance your meat intake with some bright, fresh greens. It's tangy on the front end, slightly sweet, and punctuated by a perfect crunch. It's a staple on our Curry Boys menu for this reason alone!

2 cucumbers, sliced
Pinch salt
¼ cup (60 ml) rice vinegar
2 tablespoons (24 g) palm sugar or white sugar
1 tablespoon (15 ml) lime juice
1 tablespoon (15 ml) fish sauce
1 teaspoon sesame oil
½ red onion, sliced thinly
2 Thai chilies, sliced thinly (adjust to spiciness preference)
¼ cup (4 g) chopped cilantro, plus more as needed
¼ cup (35 g) crushed roasted peanuts, plus more as needed
1 tablespoon (3 g) toasted sesame seeds, plus more as needed

1. Add cucumber slices to a medium mixing bowl. Sprinkle with a pinch of salt to reduce the moisture in cucumbers a bit. Set aside for 10 minutes and then place slices on a paper towel to dry.
2. In a medium mixing bowl, combine rice vinegar, sugar, lime juice, fish sauce, and sesame oil. Mix until sugar is dissolved.
3. In a large mixing bowl, combine cucumbers, red onion, and Thai chilies. Add salad dressing and mix, making sure everything is coated evenly. Add cilantro, roasted peanuts, and sesame seeds, and mix well. Cover bowl and refrigerate for at least 30 minutes.
4. Serve cold in small side/appetizer bowls or plates. Top with extra chopped cilantro, roasted peanuts, and sesame seeds to taste.

NOTE:
Slice cucumbers to your preference. Don't slice too thinly if you are looking for a crunchier bite.

Clockwise from top: Curry Boys BBQ Green Curry Potato Salad (page 86), Curry Boys BBQ Tangy Pickled Cucumbers (page 108), Thai-Inspired Cucumber Salad (this page)

Serves 8

CURRY BOYS BBQ GREEN CURRY POTATO SALAD

Picture this scenario: You're invited to a potluck dinner and all of your friends expect you to bring a side dish that'll blow their minds. Are you having a full-blown anxiety attack right now? Well, fear not, because we have the perfect recipe for you! This potato salad is familiar, but also novel. Comforting, yet exciting. Kids will enjoy it, and adults will speak its name into the potluck hall of fame. The real kicker is the subtle reminder of green curry paste in every creamy bite. If you're looking to take this to another level, add a bit of crispy, smoked bacon. Trust and thank us later.

For the dressing:

⅔ cups (150 g) mayonnaise (we prefer Duke's)
½ cup (120 g) Thai green curry paste
1 tablespoon (15 g) diced pickles (use dill pickles or Curry Boys BBQ Tangy Pickled Cucumbers [page 108])
2 tablespoons (20 g) diced white onion
1 tablespoon (15 ml) lime juice
1 teaspoon finely minced garlic
Pinch salt
Pinch black pepper

3 pounds (1.3 kg) potatoes (we prefer baby red potatoes)
Sprig cilantro
Pinch yellow curry powder

1. Make the dressing: In a small mixing bowl, combine all dressing ingredients.
2. Fill a medium to large pot with water and bring to a boil. Add in potatoes and boil until they are soft enough to be mashed but not falling apart, about 13 to 16 minutes, depending on the size of the pieces. Larger potatoes maybe need 20-plus minutes.
3. In a large mixing bowl, mash boiled potatoes while they are still hot. Add 1 cup (235 ml) of dressing and mix together, making sure everything is evenly coated. Consistency should be the same as creamy mashed potatoes. Cover and refrigerate for at least 1 hour. Serve cold, with a sprig of cilantro and dusted with curry powder on top!

Serves 4

SMOKED *and* CONFIT CHICKEN LEG PHỞ

Here's my hot take: Phở is a better noodle soup than ramen. Phở is comforting, light, refreshing, and just so damn good! I could honestly eat phở once a day for the rest of my life and I don't think I'd bat an eye. In fact, when I used to travel to Vietnam regularly to hang out with Andrew Ho, I'd eat it for breakfast every single day. Andrew Samia also loves phở, and this recipe is 100 percent his diabolical creation. As luscious as confit chicken can be, it is beautifully balanced by the smokiness and the aromatic herbs. Slurp it up, my dear friends. Slurp it up. —Sean

For the broth:

2 onions, peeled and halved
1 (2-inch [5 cm]) piece ginger, sliced
3 star anise
1 cinnamon stick
1 tablespoon (5 g) coriander seeds
1 tablespoon (6 g) fennel seeds
1 tablespoon (5 g) black peppercorns
2 whole chicken backs
1 tablespoon (16 g) tomato paste
3 quarts (2.8 L) water
3 cloves garlic
3 tablespoons (45 ml) fish sauce, plus more as needed
1 tablespoon (15 ml) dark soy sauce
1 tablespoon (13 g) sugar, plus more as needed

For the smoked confit chicken:

6 chicken drumsticks
2 tablespoons Curry Boys BBQ Poultry Rub (page 38)
1½ cups (355 ml) melted duck fat or extra-virgin olive oil for confit
1 cinnamon stick
3 star anise
1 tablespoon (6 g) sliced ginger
3 cloves garlic

Ingredients continued

1. Make the broth: Char the onion and ginger on the stove over an open flame for 5 minutes. In a small, dry pan, toast the star anise, cinnamon stick, coriander seeds, fennel seeds, and black peppercorns for 2 to 3 minutes, until fragrant. In a large stockpot, add the chicken backs, tomato paste, and water, and bring to a boil over high heat. Skim off any impurities that rise to the surface and then reduce the pot to a simmer. Smash garlic cloves and add them to the pot, along with the charred onion, ginger, and toasted spices. Continue to simmer for 4 hours, stirring occasionally. After simmering for 4 hours, strain the broth through a fine-mesh strainer or cheesecloth to remove the solids, then return the liquid to the pot. Season the broth with the fish sauce, dark soy sauce, and sugar. Taste the broth and adjust the seasoning by adding more fish sauce and/or sugar as needed.
2. Make the smoked confit chicken: Preheat smoker to 225°F (107°C). Liberally season the chicken drumsticks with the poultry rub. Place the drumsticks in the smoker, as far away from the fire source as possible, and smoke for 1½ to 2 hours, or until the drumsticks reach an internal temperature of 165°F (74°C) in the thickest part of the meat. Remove the drumsticks from the smoker and place them in a wide, deep pan or cast iron skillet. Add duck fat or olive oil to the pan, making sure the chicken is completely submerged in the oil. Add cinnamon stick, star anise, ginger, and garlic to the pan of submerged chicken. Gently simmer the chicken in the oil over low heat for 45 minutes. Carefully remove the drumsticks from the oil and set them aside until you are ready to assemble your bowls of phở.

Continued from previous page

For serving:

4 servings cooked rice noodles
1 jalapeño, thinly sliced
⅓ cup (16 g) thinly sliced green onion
½ cup (8 g) chopped cilantro
½ cup (20 g) whole Thai basil leaves
1 Thai chili, finely sliced
½ cup (25 g) bean sprouts
1 lime, cut into wedges
Hoisin sauce for serving
Sriracha for serving

3. Divide the cooked rice noodles between 4 bowls. Ladle the hot phở broth over the noodles. Place one chicken drumstick in each bowl. Shred the remaining 2 drumsticks from the bone and distribute the meat among the bowls. Garnish the phở with sliced jalapeño, green onion, cilantro, Thai basil, Thai chili, bean sprouts, and lime wedges. Serve with hoisin sauce and sriracha on the side.

Makes 1 QUART (946 ML)

CURRY BOYS BBQ-THAI HOUSE SALAD DRESSING

Not too long ago, we had someone ask us, "What the hell is in that salad dressing? I've been trying to re-create that umami-rich fish sauce and citrus dressing from your Thai green salad for weeks." For reasons unknown to me, I guess we never gave him the recipe. I feel bad. We have no secrets here. So, Chris, here it is! You get to have this recipe with the rest of the world! This Thai-inspired dressing is the perfect way to make any salad flavor-packed while ensuring it stays healthy. There are hints of tang and sweetness, and it ultimately ends up being an extremely refreshing and bright finish. When paired with a crunchy leafy green, you'll start to wonder if you could eat salad every day—which we wouldn't recommend, simply because you'd have no more use for this cookbook.

1½ cups (413 g) sweet chili sauce
1¼ cups (296 ml) water
½ cup (118 ml) fish sauce
½ cup (118 ml) lime juice

1. In a large mixing bowl, combine all ingredients and mix well. Serve immediately or store in the refrigerator for up to 4 to 5 days in a covered container. It is best if used within 2 to 3 days, though!

Serves 4

SMOKED CHICKEN THAI SALAD *with* ASIAN PEAR

While the BBQ and Thai curry are the stars of the show at our restaurant, the salad is not to be underestimated. It stands on its own two legs and can throw its weight around with the heaviest of hitters. It has loads of nuanced flavor and an emphasis on texture—which are two crucial elements for any great dish! —Sean

4 boneless and skinless chicken thighs
4 teaspoons (25 g) Curry Boys BBQ Poultry Rub (page 38)
16 ounces (200 g) fresh mixed greens
8 ounces (70 g) shredded green cabbage
4 Roma tomatoes, halved
2 cucumbers, sliced
½ cup (8 g) chopped cilantro
½ cup (48 g) chopped mint
½ cup (20 g) chopped Thai basil
1 Asian pear (sub 2 apples for more crunch), sliced but not too thin
½ cup (80 g) fried shallots
1 cup (235 ml) Curry Boys BBQ-Thai House Salad Dressing (page 91)

1. Preheat smoker to 225°F (107°C). Pat chicken dry and lay out on a sheet tray or cutting board. Season chicken liberally on top and bottom with the chicken rub. You'll need about 1 teaspoon of rub per chicken thigh. Place chicken onto smoker grates and smoke for 1½ to 2 hours, or until chicken has an internal temperature of 165°F (74°C). Remove chicken from smoker and rest for 10 minutes, then slice.
2. In a large mixing bowl, add fresh greens, cabbage, tomatoes, cucumbers, cilantro, mint, and Thai basil. Add 1 to 2 tablespoons (15 to 30 ml) of dressing at a time and mix, making sure everything is coated evenly. Continue until your desired dressing level is reached.
3. Top salad with sliced smoked chicken, sliced pear, and fried shallots. Enjoy with more dressing over chicken and salad if needed!

Serves 4

SMOKED BRISKET *LARB*

When I first visited Andrew Ho when he lived in Thailand, larb was literally the first thing I ate. While the salad originates from Northeast Thailand in the Isaan region, it has become so popular you can find the dish all over Thailand. I remember landing in Bangkok, calling a pink taxi, and getting dropped off in front of the Yolo Hostel on Sukhumvit Road (remember when saying "yolo" was still a thing?). I dropped my things off and immediately looked for street food. I walked maybe 50 meters and stumbled across a nice lady selling larb out of a food stall. The first bite perfectly encapsulated everything I love about Thai food: bright, pungent, spicy, and loaded with herbs. Our version uses smoked brisket, which adds a unique depth of smoke and pepper and really pairs well with the inherently bright, herbaceous notes. The beautiful thing about larb is that you can use any protein, and it will more than likely be incredible. In fact, the best version I've had in recent memory is a fried trout larb from Chef Arnold at International Market in Nashville. It's unreal how good it is. —Sean

- 2 pounds (907 g) Texas-Style Smoked Beef Brisket (can use leftovers), chopped until shredded (page 157)
- ¼ cup (60 ml) beef broth, optional
- 2 tablespoons (9 g) toasted rice powder (page 52)
- 2 teaspoons Thai chili powder or flakes (adjust to spiciness preference)
- 2 tablespoons (30 ml) fish sauce
- 2 tablespoons (30 ml) fresh lime juice
- 1 teaspoon palm sugar or brown sugar
- ½ cup (80 g) thinly sliced shallots
- ⅓ cup (16 g) chopped green onions
- ⅓ cup (5 g) chopped cilantro, plus more as needed
- ⅓ cup (32 g) whole mint leaves, plus more as needed
- ⅓ cup (13 g) chopped Thai basil, plus more as needed
- Sliced Thai chilies for garnish, optional
- 1 head iceberg or green lettuce, separated into whole leaves
- 2 cucumbers, sliced

1. Reheat chopped brisket, if needed, in a large pan over medium heat and add beef broth for moisture. Remove the pan from heat and set to the side. In an extra-large mixing bowl, combine the warm brisket, toasted rice powder, Thai chili flakes, fish sauce, lime juice, and sugar. Combine everything to ensure meat is evenly sauced. Add shallots, green onions, cilantro, mint, and Thai basil.
2. Garnish with more herbs or fresh chopped Thai chilies for a spicy kick if needed. Serve with fresh lettuce leaf wraps and cucumber slices!

Serves 4

TOM YUM SOUP with WOOD-GRILLED SHRIMP

Ladies and gentlemen—introducing the pride of Thailand! The soup of all soups! The bringer of comfort! Protector of the realm! Tom Yum Soup!

This soup is a bold, spicy, and slightly sour soup that might as well be the national soup of Thailand. It can be found all over the country—from schools to streets. Outside of Thailand, it is easily the most popular Thai soup—and arguably the most popular Thai dish in general. Our recipe is inspired by the Tom Yum soup from a restaurant in Phitsanulok, Thailand, called Tungluk—which apparently blew Andrew Ho's mind when he first had it. This version is perfectly balanced with just the right amount of sour and spicy, and an added element of charred, smoky shrimp.

4 cups (946 ml) seafood stock
2 cups (473 ml) water
4 slices galangal (sub ginger)
4 stalks lemongrass, cut into 2-inch (5 cm) pieces and smashed
4 makrut lime leaves, lightly smashed
2 cloves garlic, smashed
3 Thai chilies, sliced thinly (adjust to spiciness preference)
1 small shallot, sliced
1 cup (70 g) button mushrooms, cleaned and sliced
1 Roma tomato, cut into chunks
¼ cup (60 ml) fish sauce
1 tablespoon (15 ml) lime juice
1 tablespoon (12 g) palm sugar or brown sugar
2 tablespoons (30 g) Thai chili paste (can find at Asian market!)
1 pound (454 g) wood-grilled shrimp or prawns (see page 138, step 4)
¼ cup (4 g) chopped cilantro
¼ cup (12 g) chopped green onions
1 tablespoon (9 g) chopped red Thai chili (adjust to spiciness preference)

1. In a medium stockpot or saucepan, add seafood stock and water and bring to a low simmer. Add in galangal, lemongrass, makrut lime leaves, garlic, Thai chilies, and shallot. Bring to a low simmer for 10 minutes while stirring intermittently.
2. Add in mushrooms, tomato, fish sauce, lime juice, sugar, and Thai chili paste. Let simmer for 6 to 7 minutes, until mushrooms are soft and tender. Add in the grilled shrimp at the very end, and let simmer on low for 1 to 2 minutes to let flavors meld with shrimp—but do not overcook shrimp!
3. Ladle soup into small or medium serving bowls. Make sure some of all of the ingredients are being served in each bowl. Garnish with cilantro, green onions, and red Thai chili.

PRO TIP:
Make sure to tell guests not to eat the lemongrass, makrut lime, or galangal/ginger!

Serves **4**

TOM KHA SOUP with SMOKED CHICKEN

While Tom Yum might be the star soup that most of you have heard of, Tom Kha is your chef's favorite Thai soup. It's the unsung, unsigned, independent artist that is absolutely killing it in certain circles—but hasn't gone mainstream yet. (#IYKYK) When the temperature drops below 70°F (21°C), you already know we're thinking of snagging some of this soup because it is herbaceous, super bright, creamy, and has the soul-filling essence of a hearty chicken noodle soup.

4 boneless and skinless chicken thighs
4 teaspoons (25 g) Curry Boys BBQ Poultry Rub (page 38)
4 cups (946 ml) chicken broth
14 ounces (392 g) coconut milk
4 slices of galangal (sub ginger)
4 stalks lemongrass, cut into 2-inch (5 cm) pieces and smashed
4 makrut lime leaves, lightly smashed
2 cloves garlic, smashed
3 Thai chilies, sliced thinly (adjust to spiciness preference)
1 cup (70 g) button mushrooms, cleaned and sliced
1 Roma tomato, cut into chunks
1 shallot, sliced thinly
¼ cup (60 ml) fish sauce
1 tablespoon (15 ml) lime juice
1 tablespoon (12 g) palm sugar or brown sugar
¼ cup (4 g) chopped cilantro
4 lime wedges

1. Preheat smoker to 225°F (107°C). Pat chicken dry and lay out on a sheet tray or cutting board. Season chicken liberally on top and bottom with chicken rub. You'll need about 1 teaspoon of rub per chicken thigh. Place chicken onto smoker grates and smoke for 1½ to 2 hours, or until chicken has an internal temperature of 165°F (74°C). Remove chicken from smoker and rest for 10 minutes, then slice.
2. In a medium stockpot or saucepan, add chicken broth and coconut milk. Bring to a low simmer. Add in galangal, lemongrass, makrut lime leaves, garlic, and Thai chilies. Bring to a low simmer for 10 minutes while stirring intermittently.
3. Add in smoked chicken, mushrooms, tomato, shallot, fish sauce, lime juice, and sugar. Let simmer for 6 to 7 minutes until mushrooms are soft and tender.
4. Ladle soup into medium serving bowls. Make sure some of all of the ingredients are being served in each bowl. Garnish with cilantro and lime wedges.

PRO TIP:
Make sure to tell guests not to eat the lemongrass, makrut lime, or galangal or ginger!

Serves 4

SMOKED CHICKEN *KHAO SOI* NOODLE SOUP

Our version of this popular Northern Thai noodle soup boasts a rich coconut curry broth, perfectly smoked chicken, and crispy fried noodles for added texture. It is one of our favorite dishes for a cold day, but can honestly be enjoyed in any season. In fact, Andrew Ho once ate at the same khao soi shop in Chiang Mai, Thailand, for six meals in a row. Don't believe me? Ask Gary. Who's Gary? Don't worry about it, but he was there. Shout-out to you, Gary!

4 chicken drumsticks
4 teaspoons (25 g) Curry Boys BBQ Poultry Rub (page 38)

For the pickled mustard greens:

¼ cup (60 ml) rice vinegar
1 teaspoon white sugar
½ teaspoon salt
1 cup (100 g) chopped mustard greens
1 tablespoon (10 g) thinly sliced shallot

2 tablespoons (30 ml) vegetable oil
3 tablespoons (45 g) Thai red curry paste
1 tablespoon (6 g) Thai red curry powder
1 teaspoon turmeric powder
3 cups (710 ml) chicken broth
2 cups (448 g) unsweetened coconut milk
1 tablespoon (12 g) palm sugar or brown sugar
1 tablespoon (15 ml) fish sauce
1 teaspoon soy sauce
12 ounces (340 g) fresh or dried egg noodles, cooked
½ cup (80 g) thinly sliced red onion
½ cup (8 g) chopped cilantro
½ cup (100 g) fried egg noodles
4 lime wedges
Crispy Garlic Chili Oil (page 45), optional

1. Preheat smoker to 225°F (107°C). Pat chicken dry and lay out on a sheet tray or cutting board. Season chicken liberally all over with chicken rub. You'll need about 1 teaspoon of rub per chicken drumstick. Place chicken onto smoker grates and smoke for 2 to 2½ hours, or until internal temperature is 185°F (85°C) at the thickest part of the drumstick. Remove chicken from the smoker.
2. Make the pickled mustard greens: In a medium mixing bowl, combine rice vinegar, white sugar, and salt. Stir well until sugar and salt are dissolved. Add mustard greens and shallots, and combine to mix well. Let sit for 30 minutes in refrigerator before serving for best results!
3. In a large pot, heat oil over low to medium heat. Add in curry paste, curry powder, and turmeric powder, and sweat until fragrant, about 2 to 3 minutes. Slowly add in chicken broth and coconut milk, and stir. Add in sugar, fish sauce, and soy sauce. Simmer on medium heat for 10 minutes. Add in the smoked chicken drumsticks and simmer for 5 minutes on low heat.
4. Divide cooked noodles into 4 medium bowls. Ladle in khao soi broth over noodles and use tongs to plate the smoked chicken drumstick carefully in each bowl. Garnish each bowl with red onion, pickled mustard greens, cilantro, crispy noodles, and lime. Serve with crispy garlic chili oil if you want more of a kick!

chapter
4

ON
THE
SIDE

Makes ABOUT 1½ QUARTS (1.4 L)

VIETNAMESE-STYLE "ĐỒ CHUA" PICKLED CARROT *and* DAIKON

Pickled carrots and daikon are a versatile ingredient that can add a sweet and sour crunch to a variety of dishes. While they are a staple in Vietnamese cuisine, particularly in bánh mì and bún thịt nướng, their flavor profile complements a range of cuisines. The bright acidity and crisp texture of pickled carrots and daikon provide a perfect counterpoint to rich, smoky, or grilled proteins, and they play so well with the freshness of herbs. You can consider adding them to tacos, burgers, or rice bowls for an unexpected burst of flavor. They can also be used to brighten up a simple salad, or simply enjoyed as a tangy side dish.

2 carrots
1 daikon
2 cups (473 ml) rice vinegar
1 cup (235 ml) water
6 tablespoons (90 g) white sugar
1 tablespoon (18 g) kosher salt

1. Peel carrots and daikon and then shred or slice into matchsticks. Set aside in a bowl.
2. In a medium saucepan over medium heat, combine vinegar, water, sugar, and salt. Stir until sugar and salt are dissolved. Be careful not to boil; we just want everything to be dissolved. Remove from heat and set aside to cool.
3. To a medium-sized jar, add carrots and daikon. Top with cooled pickling liquid. Ensure the vegetables are fully submerged. Let sit in the jar at room temperature for at least 1 hour for best results. Store in an airtight container in the refrigerator for up to 2 weeks.

Pictured clockwise from top right: Filipino Pickled Green Papaya and Carrot (page 106), Vietnamese-Style "Đồ Chua" Pickled Carrot and Daikon (this page), Bread and Butter Pickled Bok Choy (page 107)

Makes ABOUT 1½ QUARTS (1.4 L)

FILIPINO PICKLED GREEN PAPAYA *and* CARROT

To all my Kuyas and Ates out there, y'all know what this recipe is about! When Andrew Ho was living in Thailand, his Filipino roommate and grilling guru, Brian Padilla, would whip this up anytime they fired up the grill. Seriously, this stuff is a game-changer, especially if you're dealing with something decadent like brisket or pork belly. It just cuts through all that richness perfectly. —Sean

1 medium or large whole unripe green papaya
1 medium-sized carrot, peeled and thinly julienned
¼ green bell pepper, core removed and thinly julienned
½ tablespoon + 1 teaspoon kosher salt, divided
2 cups (473 ml) cane vinegar
1 cup (200 g) white sugar
6 cloves garlic, thinly sliced

1. Prepare the green papaya—peel the skin, rinse under cold water, slice it in half, and scoop out the soft, white seeds. Use a mandolin with a shredding attachment and shred the flesh into fine strands (be careful!).
2. Add the shredded papaya to the julienned carrot and bell pepper in a medium-sized mixing bowl. Sprinkle with ½ tablespoon of the kosher salt and mix until well combined. Allow to brine on the counter for 30 minutes.
3. Transfer the vegetables to a colander and rinse them under cold running water for 2 minutes. Then, pour the vegetables onto a clean cheesecloth and wring out any excess moisture. Put the strained vegetables into clean glass jars.
4. Add cane vinegar, white sugar, sliced garlic, and remaining 1 teaspoon of kosher salt to a small saucepan and heat over medium heat, stirring until the mixture boils. Continue to stir over medium heat until the sugar has dissolved.
5. Carefully pour the hot liquid over the vegetables in the glass jars. Use a fork or chopsticks to stir the ingredients together. Allow the jars to rest uncovered until they have cooled to room temperature. Then, secure with lids and place in the refrigerator. Best to refrigerate for 1 to 2 days before using! Store in an airtight container in the refrigerator for up to 2 weeks.

Makes **6 TO 7 CUPS (852 TO 994 G)**

BREAD *and* BUTTER PICKLED BOK CHOY

We created this recipe for a fun restaurant collab in Portland with the fine folks at Yaowarat—a restaurant specializing in Thai Chinese food! It was meant to be an accompaniment to a brisket dish, but so many people started requesting extra servings just to enjoy on its own.

The pickled bok choy matches so well with a fatty slice of brisket over rice, or can simply be enjoyed by itself as a subtly sweet and crunchy side dish. This version of bok choy lets us know that there is still good in the world.

2 cups (473 ml) water
2 cups (473 ml) apple cider vinegar
3 cups (600 g) white sugar
1 teaspoon kosher salt
1 teaspoon mustard seeds
1 teaspoon ground turmeric
1 teaspoon celery seeds
1 teaspoon pickling spice
1 pound (454 g) whole baby bok choy (about 4 to 5 heads), root removed

1. Combine everything but the bok choy heads in a stainless steel pot and bring to a boil. Once the mixture reaches a rolling boil, turn off the heat and let it sit for 5 minutes, allowing the flavors of the spices to develop.
2. Place the baby bok choy in a large glass jar and then carefully strain the hot pickling liquid over the bok choy. Use a fork or chopsticks to stir the contents, ensuring all the bok choy is fully submerged. Let cool to room temperature before covering and refrigerating. For best flavor, use within 1 month.

Makes 2 QUARTS (1.9 L)

CURRY BOYS BBQ TANGY PICKLED CUCUMBERS

Pickles are an oft-forgotten but absolutely quintessential part of Texas barbecue. When I see them cast to the side of the plate like they're the dregs of BBQ society—I shed a single, solitary tear. I'm the kind of person who takes a bite of brisket, then takes a bite of a pickle, then takes another bite of brisket, then takes another bite of the pickle, and so on, until I'm either out of pickles or out of brisket. We prefer our pickles to be just sweet enough, just crunchy enough, and most importantly, just tangy enough. —Sean

3 English cucumbers
1⅓ cups (315 ml) apple cider vinegar
1⅓ cups (315 ml) white vinegar
5 tablespoons (65 g) granulated white sugar
1½ teaspoons kosher salt
1 tablespoon (6 g) pickling spice
½ teaspoon crushed red pepper

1. Slice the ends off the cucumbers and discard. Slice the remaining cucumbers using a mandolin (be careful!) and place them in glass jars.
2. Combine the rest of the ingredients in a medium-sized stainless steel saucepan and bring to a boil over high heat. Once the mixture is boiling, reduce the heat to medium-low and simmer for 5 minutes to allow all the spices to awaken. Strain the hot liquid over the sliced cucumbers. Allow to cool completely with the lid off, then put on the lid and store in the refrigerator for up to 2 months.

HOWDY
HOWDY
HOWDY

VIETNAMESE-STYLE GRILLED BOK CHOY

I'm going to admit something crazy: I crave bok choy more than I crave brisket. Don't tell our pitmaster, Andrew Samia, I said that. Actually, maybe, don't tell anyone I said that. Just make the recipe and you'll see why I feel this way. Charred, garlicky bok choy tossed in a sweet and tangy sauce just never gets old. It is simply a great addition to any backyard BBQ or dinner. —Sean

8 heads baby bok choy, halved lengthwise and roots removed
2 tablespoons (30 ml) vegetable oil
1 tablespoon (15 ml) lime juice
1 tablespoon (15 ml) soy sauce
1 tablespoon (15 ml) fish sauce
1 tablespoon (20 g) honey
1 clove garlic, minced
½ teaspoon black pepper
½ teaspoon Thai chili flakes (adjust to spiciness preference)
2 tablespoons (18 g) crushed roasted peanuts
2 tablespoons (20 g) fried shallots
2 tablespoons (2 g) chopped cilantro
Lime wedges

1. Wash bok choy, pat dry, and then cut in half lengthwise.
2. In a medium mixing bowl, mix together vegetable oil, lime juice, soy sauce, fish sauce, honey, garlic, black pepper, and chili flakes. Add bok choy and mix well, making sure everything is evenly coated.
3. Preheat grill to medium to high heat. Place bok choy cut-side down on grill grate and grill for 2 to 3 minutes until they are lightly charred. Flip bok choy and grill for another 1 to 2 minutes until the leaves are a bit crispy, but the stem is tender.
4. Neatly place grilled bok choy in a row on a serving platter. Serve hot and garnish with roasted peanuts, fried shallots, cilantro, and lime wedges.

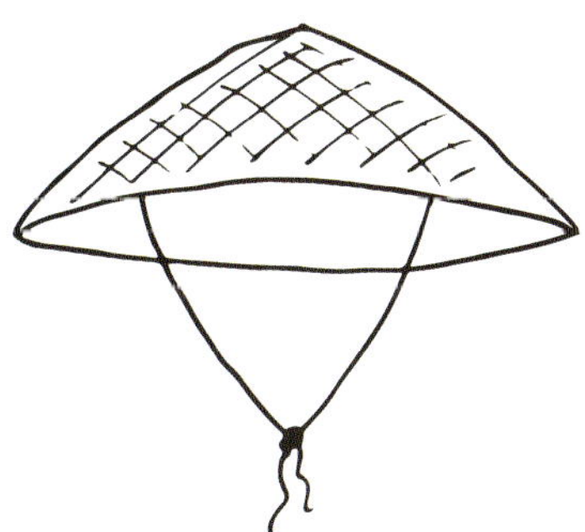

Serves 4

THAI-INSPIRED GREEN CURRY SMOKED MUSHROOMS

Do you have a dear friend who is vegetarian? Are they always longingly staring at you when you eat Texas barbecue? Do they ever ask you to describe what a tender, juicy brisket tastes like in as much detail as possible? If you answered "yes" to any of these questions, then you need to be a good friend and make them this smoked mushroom recipe. We aren't trying to create something that "tastes like meat." We simply wanted to create a recipe that stands out on its own when compared with smoked meat via a delicious marinade and a genuine smoking experience.

2 tablespoons (30 ml) vegetable oil
1 tablespoon (15 ml) lime juice
1 tablespoon (15 ml) fish sauce
1 tablespoon (15 ml) soy sauce
2 teaspoons palm sugar or brown sugar
2 cloves garlic, minced
1 teaspoon Thai green curry paste
½ teaspoon Thai chili flakes (adjust to spiciness preference)
½ teaspoon smoked paprika
1½ pounds (680 g) shiitake or portobello mushrooms
1 tablespoon (3 g) chopped green onions
1 tablespoon (1 g) chopped cilantro
1 tablespoon (3 g) chopped Thai basil

1. In a large mixing bowl, combine vegetable oil, lime juice, fish sauce, soy sauce, sugar, garlic, green curry paste, chili flakes, and paprika. Add in mushrooms and mix well, making sure everything is evenly coated. Let marinade for at least 15 minutes.
2. Preheat smoker to 225°F (107°C). Place mushrooms on smoker grate, spreading them out so they are not touching. Smoke for 50 to 60 minutes, flipping halfway through until mushrooms are a bit shriveled and have a nice brown color.
3. Neatly plate mushrooms in a serving bowl or plate and garnish with green onions, cilantro, and Thai basil. This is a delicious option for vegetarians and those looking for a lighter BBQ meal!

PRO TIP:
We recommend shiitake or portobello mushrooms, but you can use a nicer mushroom if you want! You can also use yellow or red curry paste instead.

Serves 4 TO 6

STIR-FRIED GREEN BEANS *with* SMOKED *MINCED PORK*

Growing up, Andrew Ho and I used to go to this Chinese/Vietnamese restaurant called Tan Tan in Houston's Chinatown. If you are an Asian living in Houston, you know the restaurant I'm talking about. If you aren't Asian, or from Houston, go check out the restaurant if you get a chance! One dish that consistently graces the tables of most guests is a simple yet flavorful stir-fried green bean medley. Honestly, those green beans are always reliable, and with so many dishes coming and going in our lives, they're a steady, comforting presence. Our recipe, with its Texas barbecue twist, pays homage to that beloved classic, capturing the essence of those cherished memories and the vibrant flavors of our upbringing. —Sean

For the stir-fry sauce:

1 tablespoon (8 g) cornstarch
2 tablespoons (30 ml) water
2 tablespoons (30 ml) soy sauce
1 tablespoon (16 g) hoisin sauce
1 tablespoon (19 g) oyster sauce
1 tablespoon (15 ml) rice vinegar
1 tablespoon (15 g) sriracha (adjust to spiciness preference)
1 teaspoon white sugar

1 pound (454 g) green beans, ends trimmed
½ pound (227 g) smoked minced or ground pork
2 tablespoons (30 ml) vegetable oil
1 white onion, sliced thinly
4 cloves garlic, minced
2 tablespoons (12 g) minced ginger
1 red bell pepper, sliced into strips
2 tablespoons (20 g) fried shallots

1. Make the stir-fry sauce: In a small mixing bowl, mix cornstarch and water. In a separate small mixing bowl, combine the rest of the sauce ingredients. Slowly stir the sauce and pour in the cornstarch slurry mix. Set aside.
2. Bring a large pot of water to a boil. Add green beans and let boil for 2 to 3 minutes until they are slightly tender but still have a crunch to them. Quickly drain the green beans and run them under cold water or plunge into an ice bath to cool down. Drain and set aside.
3. Preheat smoker to 200°F (93°C). Line a medium-sized baking tray with foil. Spread out the pork on the tray so that the smoke can penetrate the meat nicely. Smoke for 35 to 45 minutes or until pork reaches an internal temperature of 160°F (71°C). Set aside, uncovered, to cool down slightly. The pork will be cooked more in the next step.
4. In a large wok or saucepan, heat up vegetable oil on medium to high heat. Add in pork and stir for 3 to 4 minutes, making sure to separate the pork so the meat gets crispy with a golden brown color. Add in white onion, garlic, ginger, and red pepper. Stir-fry for 4 to 5 minutes. Add green beans to the wok and stir to combine everything. Pour the stir-fry sauce evenly over the green beans and pork and stir-fry well, making sure everything is coated. Cook for 2 to 3 minutes until sauce begins to thicken.
5. On a large serving platter, plate green beans and pork and garnish with crispy fried shallots! Goes great with jasmine rice or our ribs.

Makes **1 PAN, 9 X 9 X 2-INCH (23 X 23 X 5 CM), TO SERVE 8**

RED CURRY CORN BREAD

Honestly, it's a real treat when corn bread pops up at a BBQ. It's the fluffy, buttery cloud to BBQ's meaty thunder. This corn bread recipe is everything you want in a slightly sweet, slightly salty snack. The addition of red curry elevates the dish with a subtle warmth and depth, creating a more complex and intriguing flavor profile that will keep you coming back for more.

Butter or vegetable oil to grease pan
1 cup (125 g) all-purpose flour
1 cup (140 g) yellow cornmeal
1 tablespoon (14 g) baking powder
¼ cup (60 g) brown sugar
½ teaspoon salt
2 eggs
1 cup (235 ml) buttermilk
½ cup (112 g) unsalted butter, melted
½ cup (112 g) coconut milk
1 tablespoon (15 g) Thai red curry paste
1 tablespoon (15 ml) fish sauce, optional
½ cup (63 g) corn kernels, fresh or frozen
1 Thai chili pepper, sliced (adjust for spiciness preference)
Whole cilantro leaves for garnish

1. Preheat oven to 400°F (204°C). Grease a standard 9-inch (23 cm) baking dish with butter or vegetable oil. Place the dish in the oven to get hot.
2. In a large mixing bowl, whisk together flour, cornmeal, baking powder, sugar, and salt.
3. In a separate large mixing bowl, whisk together eggs, buttermilk, melted butter, coconut milk, red curry paste, and fish sauce until combined well. Slowly mix in corn kernels and Thai chili.
4. Slowly mix the dry ingredients into the wet ingredients, mixing well until combined. Note that the batter does not need to be completely incorporated. Pour batter into the preheated and oiled baking dish.
5. Bake for 22 to 25 minutes or until corn bread is golden brown. When a toothpick is inserted, it should come out like butter. Let sit for 10 minutes before slicing into squares to serve. Serve hot on small plates with whole cilantro leaves for color. Pairs great with our brisket, sausage, or ribs!

Makes **12 BISCUITS**

VIET-TEXAN-STYLE SPICY GREEN ONION CHEDDAR BAY BISCUITS

Although the glory days of Red Lobster seem to be past us, their Cheddar Bay biscuits will forever be elite in my mind; for that reason alone, I hope to the Gods that they never go out of business. But if they do, we've got a pretty spectacular version that cranks the flavors, and the heat, up a notch with our savory biscuit glaze. —Sean

2 cups (250 g) all-purpose flour
1 tablespoon (14 g) baking powder
½ teaspoon baking soda
1 teaspoon sugar
½ teaspoon kosher salt
½ teaspoon black pepper
½ teaspoon garlic powder
½ teaspoon Thai chili flakes
1 cup (115 g) shredded sharp cheddar cheese
½ cup (24 g) thinly sliced green onions, white and green parts
¼ cup (56 g) unsalted butter, cubed
¾ cup (177 ml) cold buttermilk

For the biscuit glaze:

3 tablespoons (42 g) unsalted butter
1 clove garlic, minced finely
1 tablespoon (3 g) finely chopped green onions, only the green part
½ teaspoon fish sauce
½ teaspoon lime juice

1. Preheat oven to 425°F (218°C). Line a baking sheet with parchment paper.
2. In a large mixing bowl, whisk together flour, baking powder, baking soda, sugar, kosher salt, black pepper, garlic powder, and Thai chili flakes. Mix in shredded cheese and sliced green onions. Cut in butter until it is 95 percent mixed in, leaving small pieces of unmelted butter.
3. Add buttermilk into the dry mix. Carefully mix until a rough and lumpy texture forms. You do not want to overmix this!
4. Use a ¼-cup (60 ml) measuring scoop to scoop 12 portions of dough onto the parchment paper–lined tray. Bake for about 15 minutes or until tops of biscuits are golden.
5. Make the biscuit glaze: Melt butter in a small saucepan over low heat. Mix in garlic and green onions, and cook for 1 to 2 minutes until herbs become fragrant. Make sure not to burn garlic! Mix in fish sauce and lime juice and stir until everything is combined.
6. Serve biscuits hot out of the oven brushed with the garlic butter biscuit glaze. These go great with a rack of ribs or grilled wings!

Serves 4

GRILLED BROCCOLINI *with* *THAI* CHILI GARLIC SAUCE

Broccoli is great. Broccolini is greater. The florets get charred beautifully when grilled, and the tender stems make for an easy bite. Most importantly, it is super versatile, because the flavor is simply milder and easier to manage. This recipe allows the broccolini to lead the band, as it is accompanied by a chorus of background singers disguised as a sweet and garlicky Thai-inspired sauce. It's simple on its own, but can also be a wonderful side if you have some hearty smoked meats nearby.

2 bunches broccolini
1 tablespoon (15 ml) vegetable oil
Pinch kosher salt
8 cloves garlic, chopped
4 Thai chilies, finely sliced
6 tablespoons (114 g) oyster sauce
4 teaspoons (16 g) palm sugar or brown sugar
¼ cup (60 ml) fish sauce

1. Prepare your grill for high heat by building a high bed of burned-down wood or lump charcoal.
2. Toss broccolini with vegetable oil and kosher salt, then grill it directly over the coals for 2 to 3 minutes per side. Remove broccolini from the grill, chop into pieces roughly 2 inches (5 cm) long, and set aside in a medium mixing bowl.
3. Using a mortar and pestle, roughly crush garlic and chilies. Add crushed garlic and chilies, oyster sauce, sugar, and fish sauce to the mixing bowl with the grilled broccolini. Toss everything together until all the ingredients are fully incorporated.
4. Heat a sauté pan over high heat until the pan starts to smoke, then add the contents of the mixing bowl to the pan and sauté over high heat for 2 minutes. Transfer to a serving platter and enjoy!

Serves 4

TAO JIEW–GLAZED SMOKED EGGPLANT

Vegetables should get more love on the smoker. Eggplant in particular is amazing when smoked. The tao jiew—Thai fermented soybean paste—gives these eggplant halves a deeply savory, funky, and misolike flavor profile that can compete with any meat out there. The smoking process imparts a subtle smokiness that permeates the eggplant's flesh, creating a tender, almost creamy texture that contrasts beautifully with the intense savoriness of the tao jiew glaze. This dish is a testament to the transformative power of smoking, proving that vegetables can indeed take center stage on the smoker.

2 large Chinese eggplants
1 teaspoon kosher salt
2 tablespoons (30 ml) vegetable oil, divided
1 clove garlic, finely minced
½ teaspoon grated ginger
1 tablespoon (16 g) tao jiew
1 tablespoon (15 ml) dark soy sauce
2 teaspoons palm sugar or brown sugar
1 teaspoon lime juice
1 tablespoon (15 ml) Crispy Garlic Chili Oil (page 45)
2 tablespoons (30 ml) water
2 tablespoons (18 g) crushed peanuts
2 tablespoons (2 g) chopped cilantro
1 lime, quartered

1. Slice the eggplants lengthwise and shallowly score the flesh in a crisscross pattern. Sprinkle the flesh of the eggplants with kosher salt and allow them to sit for 15 minutes to draw out excess moisture. Pat the eggplants dry with a paper towel and then brush 1 tablespoon (15 ml) of vegetable oil onto the flesh.
2. Preheat your smoker to 250°F (121°C). Place the halved eggplants in the smoker, cut-side up, as far away from the fire source as possible. Smoke for 45 minutes.
3. While the eggplant is smoking, prepare your glaze. Add the remaining 1 tablespoon (15 ml) of vegetable oil to a small saucepan over medium heat. Add garlic and ginger and sauté for about 30 seconds or until fragrant. Add tao jiew, dark soy sauce, sugar, lime juice, crispy garlic chili oil, and water to the saucepan. Gently simmer for 3 minutes to slightly thicken the sauce.
4. Prepare your grill for high heat by building a high bed of burned-down wood or lump charcoal. Liberally brush the glaze over both sides of the smoked eggplant and grill over high heat. Flip and brush with more glaze every 30 seconds or so to caramelize the glaze on both sides, 4 total flips. Remove the eggplant from the grill and garnish with crushed peanuts and chopped cilantro. Serve with lime wedges.

Makes **2 QUARTS (1.9 L), TO SERVE 8 TO 12**

CURRY BOYS BBQ CURRY CREAMED CORN

Creamed corn is a Texas barbecue staple, and our version reigns supreme at Curry Boys BBQ. It remains at the top of the sales charts due to its absolutely indulgent energy. When you're craving something bad, but also want it to be worth the "badness," then look no further. The recipe results in a perfectly creamy consistency while the Madras curry powder adds a unique blend of spice and a touch of heat. We make a big batch here because this dish is a crowd-pleaser at parties and potlucks, but you can, of course, reduce the quantities.

5 cups (650 g) frozen corn kernels
1 pound (454 g) cream cheese
1 cup (200 g) white sugar
3 tablespoons (27 g) granulated garlic
2 tablespoons (14 g) granulated onion
2 tablespoons (12 g) Cajun seasoning
2 tablespoons (12 g) chicken bouillon powder
4 teaspoons (9 g) black pepper
1 teaspoon Madras yellow curry powder
2 tablespoons (2 g) chopped cilantro

1. Bring a medium or large pot of water to a boil. Add frozen corn and boil for 5 minutes. Pour corn into a strainer and let drain to dry for 15 minutes. Set aside.
2. Put a large empty pot over low to medium heat. Add in cream cheese and heat until softened. Add corn in with cream cheese and stir well. Make sure all corn kernels are covered with melted cream cheese. Add in sugar, granulated garlic, granulated onion, Cajun seasoning, chicken bouillon, and black pepper. Stir well to ensure everything is combined.
3. To serve, plate in small side bowls and top with a touch of Madras curry powder. Garnish with chopped cilantro. Goes great with any of our brisket dishes!

chapter
5

SEAFOOD AND VEGGIE MAINS

BBQ
TOFU

Serves 6

COLD *CHILI GARLIC* NOODLES

My parents used to take me to a church near Houston's Chinatown/Asia Town area, and the only thing I'd ever look forward to was going to a dim sum palace after church. We'd typically go if there was a special occasion or someone was visiting from out of town. So whenever I knew someone was visiting, I'd purposely skip breakfast to give myself more room for dim sum delights. As a kid, I only really enjoyed three or four dishes: har gow (crystal dumplings), char siu bao (steamed BBQ pork buns), si yao wong (soy sauce chow mein), and those orange slices you'd get at the end of the meal. (I once proudly boasted at the table that I had eaten fifteen orange slices—but no one seemed to care about my amazing feat.) My absolute favorite was the soy sauce chow mein, and this recipe is inspired by those bold flavors. The noodles are perfectly chewy, with just enough bite, and the sauce has just enough heat and sweetness to it. We love finishing the dish with a crunch from some fried shallots. —Sean

1 pound (454 g) egg noodles (look for a Chinese brand)
6 tablespoons (89 ml) low-sodium soy sauce
2 tablespoons (30 ml) water
2 tablespoons (30 g) sriracha
¼ cup (50 g) white sugar
2 teaspoons + 3 tablespoons (27 g) Crispy Garlic Chili Oil (page 45), divided
3 tablespoons (3 g) chopped cilantro
3 tablespoons (30 g) fried shallots

1. Prepare the noodles according to the package instructions. You'll probably need to boil egg noodles for about 4 minutes until cooked but not soft or mealy. Strain and run under cold water. Set aside in a large mixing bowl.
2. In a medium mixing bowl, combine soy sauce, water, sriracha, white sugar, and 2 teaspoons of the crispy garlic chili oil. Stir well.
3. Pour sauce evenly over noodles and mix well, making sure all noodles are evenly coated. Using tongs, plate noodles in a small bowl or plate. Neatly garnish with cilantro, fried shallots, and the remaining chili crunch.

Serves 4

SMOKED TOFU *DRUNKEN NOODLES*

We love a wide noodle that has the perfect bouncy, chewy bite, and that just so happens to be one of the defining characteristics of drunken noodles—a crowd favorite in Thailand and in Western countries. The other defining characteristic in our version of this recipe is the smoked tofu stir-fried in the slightly sweet, soy-based sauce. Tofu is severely underrated and Asians have been killing it in the tofu game for years. When cooked properly, it's a texture bomb that takes on the flavor of whatever you're cooking it in, so in this case, you know it'll taste amazing. You may also be wondering where this dish gets its name from. The "mao" in pad khee mao, the Thai name for this dish, translates to "drunk," and although there are many variations of the origin, ranging from "the sauce is so good, it'll get you drunk" to "the flavors are great after you've been drinking all night," we like to think it means "a drunk noodle speaks a sober heart's craving."

1 pound (454 g) extra-firm tofu
2 tablespoons (30 ml) soy sauce
1 tablespoon (15 ml) dark soy sauce
1 tablespoon (12 g) palm sugar or brown sugar
1 teaspoon onion powder
1 teaspoon garlic powder
½ teaspoon white pepper
4 tablespoons (60 ml) vegetable oil, divided

For the sauce:

3 tablespoons (57 g) oyster sauce
2 tablespoons (30 ml) soy sauce
1 tablespoon (15 ml) dark soy sauce
1 tablespoon (15 ml) fish sauce
1 tablespoon (12 g) palm sugar or brown sugar
1 teaspoon white pepper

Ingredients continued

1. Preheat smoker to 225°F (107°C). Drain the tofu block and dry it with paper towels. You want to get rid of as much moisture as possible. Slice the tofu block in half, parallel with your cutting board, to make 2 half-thickness pieces.
2. In a small mixing bowl, combine and mix soy sauce, dark soy sauce, sugar, onion powder, garlic powder, white pepper, and 1 tablespoon (15 ml) of vegetable oil.
3. Brush tofu with seasoning mixture until liberally and evenly coated. Place tofu pieces on smoker grates, making sure they are not touching. Smoke for 1 hour to 1 hour and 20 minutes, flipping halfway through, until they have a nice brown color. Remove tofu from smoker and let cool. Slice into 1-inch (2.5 cm) cubes and set to the side.
4. Make the sauce: In a small mixing bowl, combine all sauce ingredients. Set to the side.

Continued

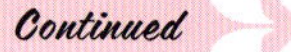

Continued from previous page

4 cloves garlic, minced
3 Thai chilies, minced (adjust to spiciness preference)
1 red bell pepper, sliced
1 white onion, sliced
1 cup (90 g) baby bok choy, sliced at the base (sub spinach leaves)
8 ounces (227 g) or 4 servings extra-wide cooked rice noodles
1¼ cups (50 g) Thai basil leaves, divided
8 lime wedges
¼ cup (4 g) chopped cilantro
Thai chili powder or flakes

5. In a large wok or pan, heat the remaining 3 tablespoons (45 ml) of vegetable oil on medium to high heat. Add garlic and Thai chilies and sauté for 30 seconds. (Make sure not to burn the garlic!) Add in bell pepper, white onion, and baby bok choy and cook for 2 to 3 minutes until vegetables are slightly cooked and soft. Add in smoked tofu cubes and cook for another 1 to 2 minutes.
6. Slide everything to one side of the wok. Add in rice noodles and sauce and begin stirring and cooking everything together. Make sure to continue stir-frying for 3 to 4 minutes until noodles have absorbed the sauce and everything is mixed and coated evenly. Add in 1 cup (40 g) of Thai basil leaves. Stir for 20 seconds and then cut heat.
7. Divide onto 4 plates and garnish with lime wedges, the remaining ¼ cup (10 g) of Thai basil leaves, chopped cilantro, and Thai chili flakes!

PRO TIP:

When cooking the noodles, make sure the pan doesn't get too crowded so that the noodles can char properly. You also want to let the noodles sit in the sauce for a little bit to really get that flavorful char on the noodle.

Serves 8

VIET-CAJUN-STYLE GARLIC BUTTER SEAFOOD BOIL *with* SMOKED SAUSAGE, SHRIMP, MUSSELS, *and* CRAWFISH

Nothing on earth brings together family and friends like a crawfish boil. In fact, we're almost certain the word "community" comes from the old Native American word for crawfish. Don't quote us on this. In all seriousness, crawfish is more than food for us. It goes beyond that. It's cheerful bonhomie. It's family. It's community. I grew up going to Viet-Cajun crawfish boils as a kid in Houston, and quite honestly, they will always be some of my fondest memories. The inevitable cultural mix of Viet-Cajun is a story of survival, adaptation, and, ultimately, damn good food. For the uninformed, many Vietnamese immigrants came to Houston after the fall of Saigon in 1975, and through the decades, have formed their own style of cuisine that has since been cemented in Houston's culinary legacy. What once began as backyard boils has evolved into full-blown restaurants all over the city specializing and celebrating the cultural triumph that is equal parts Vietnam and Gulf Coast.

Most people don't know this, but I became great friends with Andrew Ho because he used to throw crawfish boils at his house when we were in college. What's even crazier is that before Andrew Ho and I started our first restaurant together in 2017, we threw one of our first pop-up crawfish boil events at a BBQ restaurant that Andrew Samia owned, and we became close friends after the event. Crawfish is community, and I will forever die on that hill. —Sean

For the garlic butter sauce:

¼ pound (113 g) unsalted butter
2 cups (473 ml) orange juice
2 cups (473 ml) water
2½ tablespoons (15 g) Cajun or seafood boil seasoning
1 teaspoon chicken bouillon powder
½ cup (60 g) brown sugar
1 teaspoon cayenne pepper
1 teaspoon paprika powder
½ cup (75 g) fresh minced garlic

Ingredients continued

1. Make the garlic butter sauce: Place a medium saucepan over medium heat and add all sauce ingredients except garlic. Mix well and bring to a boil. Once the sauce is boiling, add minced garlic and let simmer on low heat for 2 to 3 minutes.

Continued

Continued from previous page

1¼ cups (120 g) Cajun or seafood boil seasoning, divided
2 cups (473 ml) orange juice
2 whole oranges, halved
2 pounds (907 g) (about 8) baby red potatoes
8 smoked andouille sausage links
4 ears corn, cut into halves
2 pounds (907 g) live crawfish (see tip)
2 pounds (907 g) shell-on shrimp, head on or off
2 pounds (907 g) fresh and cleaned mussels (sub frozen)
½ cup (24 g) thinly sliced green onions
Cayenne pepper, optional (adjust to spiciness preference)

2. Fill a large pot with water and bring it to a boil. Add 1 cup (96 g) of Cajun seasoning, orange juice, and oranges. Mix until Cajun seasoning is dissolved. Drop your empty strainer basket into the pot. Toss potatoes into the pot and boil for 10 to 12 minutes. Toss in sausage, corn, and crawfish, and boil for 5 minutes. Toss in shrimp and mussels, boiling for about 3 minutes until shrimp look pink and mussels open up (if live).
3. With a glove or towel, lift basket out of the water, allow to drain, and pour the food into a large bowl or cooler. Be careful not to let the vapor burn your hands or face! Pour or ladle the garlic butter sauce over the boiled seafood medley. Toss everything together to make sure it's all coated evenly.
4. Serve hot on individual plates or over butcher paper on a long table. Garnish with chopped green onions and the remaining Cajun seasoning. Sprinkle with cayenne pepper if you want an extra kick!

PRO TIPS:

You'll need a large stockpot, a matching strainer basket, and a fryer or burner base, like what you fry a turkey in.

Make sure to wash and purge your crawfish before cooking! Soak your live crawfish in salt water for 10 minutes and then rinse with fresh water before adding to the boil.

Serves 4

THAI-STYLE BBQ SHRIMP *with Penang Curry Butter on* TOASTED BAGUETTE

New Orleans—the city that has stolen our hearts and taste buds! It's been a culinary inspiration for us, and we've collaborated with some amazing chefs there (shout-out to Chef Amarys and Chef Jordan). In fact, our pitmaster, Andrew Samia, married his beautiful wife in New Orleans! Inspired by all this deliciousness, we've whipped up our own Thai-inspired version of New Orleans BBQ shrimp. (Although the original dish is called "BBQ shrimp" in New Orleans, it's not actually barbecued.) The Penang curry–toasted baguette is an absolute diabolical combination as well. Who can resist a little culinary mischief?

3 pounds (1.4 kg) large shell-on shrimp
1 tablespoon (6 g) Cajun or seafood boil seasoning
1 tablespoon (6 g) ground white pepper
6 tablespoons (84 g) unsalted butter, softened, divided
½ tablespoon Thai Penang curry paste
2 tablespoons (30 ml) vegetable oil, divided
¼ cup (40 g) chopped onions
2 tablespoons (20 g) minced garlic
2 stalks lemongrass, smashed and chopped
1 Thai chili, finely chopped
3 tablespoons (45 ml) fish sauce
2 tablespoons (38 g) oyster sauce
1 tablespoon (12 g) palm sugar or brown sugar
¼ cup (60 ml) dry vermouth
2 cups (473 ml) water
1 large French-style baguette
2 cups (448 g) coconut milk
½ cup (20 g) roughly chopped fresh Thai basil leaves
1 tablespoon (15 ml) lime juice
1 tablespoon (1 g) chopped cilantro

1. Peel the shrimp, leaving only the tails attached. Add to a bowl and season with Cajun spice and ground white pepper. Set the shells aside, and refrigerate the shrimp to marinate.
2. Add ¼ cup (56 g) of softened butter and Penang curry paste to a food processor and blend until well incorporated.
3. Heat 1 tablespoon (15 ml) of vegetable oil in a large pot over high heat. Add onions, garlic, lemongrass, and Thai chili. Sauté for 1 to 2 minutes until fragrant. Add reserved shrimp shells, fish sauce, oyster sauce, sugar, dry vermouth, and water. Stir well and bring to a boil. Once boiling, turn down the heat and simmer for 30 minutes. Remove from heat, let cool for 10 minutes, then strain the sauce base into a small saucepan. Bring the strained sauce to a boil and cook until it thickens into a syrupy consistency, about 15 minutes.
4. Preheat oven to 375°F (191°C). Slice your French-style baguette in half, lengthwise. Spread the Penang curry compound butter over both slices of bread. Toast in the oven until golden brown, about 8 minutes. Remove the dish from the oven and set it aside.
5. Heat the remaining 1 tablespoon (15 ml) of oil in a large skillet over high heat. Sear the seasoned shrimp for about 1 to 2 minutes on each side, until shrimp turn pink and opaque. Add the reduced sauce and coconut milk to the skillet, stirring to combine. Reduce the heat and simmer for 3 minutes.
6. Remove shrimp from the skillet and whisk the remaining 2 tablespoons (28 g) of butter into the sauce. Stir in Thai basil and lime juice.
7. Divide the shrimp onto 4 plates. Spoon the sauce over the shrimp and garnish with chopped cilantro and a slice of toasted baguette.

Serves 4

WOOD-GRILLED *THAI PRAWNS* *with* GARLIC-HERB SAUCE

The first restaurant that Andrew Ho and I opened was an Asian-inspired seafood boil restaurant because we honestly couldn't find a spot in San Antonio that prepared seafood the way we liked. And although our restaurant was primarily focused on Viet-Cajun seafood boils, we also had a lot of Thai influence on the menu due to Ho living and working in Thailand for many years. This recipe was inspired by a Laotian chef of ours (shout-out to Kap) and we ran it as a special in the early days. In the restaurant, the prawns technically weren't wood-grilled, but the honest truth is, they taste way better with that mild, clean smoke from a dried and cured wood. If you are a seafood enthusiast like us, then you'll appreciate this recipe for all of its well-seasoned and charred glory. —Sean

8 cloves garlic
¾ teaspoon white peppercorns
1 bunch cilantro stems, roughly chopped
2½ teaspoons oyster sauce
1½ teaspoons fish sauce
1½ teaspoons palm sugar or brown sugar
2 tablespoons (30 ml) water
1½ teaspoons shrimp paste in oil
1½ pounds (680 g) jumbo shell-on prawns, cleaned and deveined
1 tablespoon (15 ml) vegetable oil
Pinch kosher salt
2 tablespoons (28 g) unsalted butter
1 lime, cut into 8 wedges
2 tablespoons (2 g) cilantro, roughly chopped
¼ cup (40 g) fried shallots

1. Add garlic cloves to a mortar and crush with a pestle until chunky. Remove seven-eighths of the crushed garlic and set it aside for later use. Make an herb paste by adding white peppercorns and cilantro stems to the remaining crushed garlic in the mortar, and continue to pound everything into a paste. Set aside.
2. Make the sauce by combining the oyster sauce, fish sauce, sugar, water, and shrimp paste in a small mixing bowl, whisking together until the sugar is dissolved. Set aside.
3. Prepare your grill for medium-high heat by spreading out a bed of burned-down wood or lump charcoal.
4. Prepare the prawns for grilling by patting them dry with a paper towel, then toss them with vegetable oil and salt. Grill the prawns directly over the coals on the grate for 3 minutes, then flip and grill for an additional 2 to 3 minutes, or until they turn opaque and are lightly charred. Be careful not to overcook the prawns! Remove the prawns from the grill and set aside.
5. Melt butter in a sauté pan over medium heat. Add reserved crushed garlic to the melted butter and sauté for 2 minutes over medium heat. Add herb paste mixture to the crushed garlic and butter, and continue sautéing for 30 seconds, or until fragrant. Pour the sauce from earlier into the garlic and herb paste mixture in the sauté pan, increase the heat to high, and stir for 1 minute to slightly reduce.
6. Turn off the heat and add the grilled prawns to the pan. Toss them in the pan sauce for 30 seconds to coat well. Using tongs, transfer prawns to a serving platter and spoon the pan sauce over them. Garnish the platter with lime wedges, chopped cilantro, and fried shallots.

Serves 6

WOOD-GRILLED WHOLE RED SNAPPER *with* THAI SEAFOOD SAUCE

A whole roasted fish might be a crazy sight to many folks, but for many Asians, it is just another dish at a family party or holiday event. Red snapper is a great fish to grill because of its mild, semisweet, and nutty flavor—which makes it an easy crowd-pleaser. For this recipe, we stuff the snapper with lemongrass to allow it to steam inside the grilled fish while the seasoned skin gets nice and firm. At the very end, we like to coat the fish in a delicious, pungent, and citrus-forward sauce. It will be a guaranteed showstopper.

6 Thai chilies, thinly sliced
4 cloves garlic, finely minced
10 cilantro stems, finely chopped
4 teaspoons (16 g) palm sugar or brown sugar
¼ cup (60 ml) fish sauce
5 tablespoons (74 ml) lime juice
2 whole red snappers, about 3 pounds (1.3 kg) each
6 stalks lemongrass
1 cup (300 g) kosher salt
2 tablespoons (16 g) all-purpose flour
1 tablespoon (15 ml) water
2 Thai chilies, thinly sliced
½ cup (8 g) whole cilantro leaves
½ cup (20 g) whole Thai basil leaves
2 tablespoons (20 g) fried shallots

1. Prepare your seafood sauce by crushing the sliced Thai chilies, minced garlic, chopped cilantro stems, and sugar with a mortar and pestle until they form a paste. Then add the fish sauce and lime juice, and swirl together. Set aside.
2. Prepare your grill for low heat by spreading a thin, even layer of burned-down wood or charcoal.
3. While the grill is heating, prepare your fish by rinsing them under cold water and then patting dry with paper towels.
4. Bruise the stalks of lemongrass by hitting them with the back of a chef's knife or a rolling pin. Then, stuff 3 stalks of lemongrass in each of the 2 snappers.
5. In a mixing bowl, combine the kosher salt, all-purpose flour, and water. Mix this up nicely with your hands to form a paste, and then coat each fish thoroughly with the mixture.
6. Grill the fish over low heat; you need to slow-cook the fish's flesh without burning the outside, so make sure to keep your bed of coals low and spread out. Grill the fish for 20 minutes and then flip. Continue grilling the fish on the other side until it feels firm, approximately 15 to 20 minutes more.
7. Remove the fish from the grill and arrange on a serving platter. To serve, use a knife to cut through the skin of the fish, which should then lift cleanly off, revealing the moist and flaky meat inside. You can serve the seafood sauce on the side for dipping, or spoon it directly onto the fish. Garnish your platter of whole, grilled fish with thinly sliced Thai chilies, whole leaves of cilantro and Thai basil, and a sprinkle of fried shallots for added texture!

chapter
6

CHICKEN AND DUCK MAINS

Serves 8

PEPPERY SMOKED CHICKEN *and* THAI YELLOW CURRY *with* ROASTED GREEN BEANS *and* BELL PEPPERS

Smoked chicken doesn't get enough love in the Texas barbecue world, but I'm here to tell you that smoked chicken thigh is arguably more elite and approachable than any other smoked protein! Now before anyone asks, Asians love dark meat. We exclusively use dark meat at home, and it's simply because there is more fat and more flavor. Who wouldn't want that?! When you pair our smoked, juicy chicken thigh with our earthy yellow curry, you have yourself one of the coziest and most comforting dishes that you can eat regularly!

- 8 boneless and skinless chicken thighs
- 2 tablespoons + 2 teaspoons (17 g) Curry Boys BBQ Poultry Rub (page 38)
- 2 tablespoons (30 ml) vegetable oil
- 2 teaspoons fish sauce
- 1 teaspoon garlic powder
- 1 teaspoon turmeric powder
- 1 teaspoon palm sugar or brown sugar
- ½ teaspoon white pepper
- 2 cups (200 g) green beans, cut to your preference
- 2 yellow bell peppers, sliced
- 2 red bell peppers, sliced
- 2¼ quarts (2.1 L) Thai Yellow Curry Sauce (page 26)
- 8 servings cooked Thai jasmine rice
- ¼ cup (40 g) fried shallots
- ¼ cup (4 g) chopped cilantro
- ¼ cup (10 g) chopped Thai basil
- Chili oil, optional
- Curry Boys BBQ Tangy Pickled Cucumbers (page 108), optional

1. Preheat smoker to 225°F (107°C). Pat chicken dry and lay out on a sheet tray or cutting board. Season chicken liberally on top and bottom with chicken rub. You'll need about 1 teaspoon of rub per chicken thigh. Place chicken onto smoker grates and smoke for 1½ to 2 hours, or until chicken measures an internal temperature of 165°F (74°C). Remove from smoker and let rest for 10 minutes. Slice.
2. Preheat oven to 400°F (204°C). Grease a baking sheet.
3. In a large mixing bowl, combine vegetable oil, fish sauce, garlic powder, turmeric powder, sugar, and white pepper. Add in green beans and bell peppers and mix well, making sure everything is evenly coated. Spread vegetables out on baking sheet so they are not touching. Roast for 12 to 15 minutes, flipping halfway through until vegetables are lightly browned and caramelized, but still have good color.
4. Warm the Thai yellow curry sauce in a pan over medium heat. Add in roasted vegetables while stirring and bring curry to a low simmer. Curry is ready.
5. To serve, scoop a portion of jasmine rice into one side of a medium to large serving bowl. Pour one ladle of yellow curry and vegetables onto the empty side of the bowl. Add one sliced smoked chicken thigh on top of the yellow curry and vegetables, and then ladle extra curry sauce over the chicken. Garnish with fried shallots, cilantro, and Thai basil. Serve with chili oil and house pickles if you're wanting an extra flavor bomb!

Serves 8

SMOKED CURRY CHICKEN SALAD SANDWICHES

This smoked curry chicken salad sandwich is a popular special that I honestly wish was a full-time menu item at Curry Boys BBQ. Grace and Kyla, our amazing general managers, have an inside joke that everyone is actively plotting against me to make sure it doesn't end up on the menu permanently, so I'm forced to live a miserable life. Look, I get it. We don't always have the ingredients necessary to make it, but that doesn't mean our incredible guests shouldn't get to consistently experience this smoky, creamy sandwich punctuated by a tangy pickle! I'm hoping someone who reads this is willing to start a petition with me. —Sean

2 pounds (907 g) boneless and skinless chicken thighs
8 teaspoons (17 g) Curry Boys BBQ Poultry Rub (page 38)

For the dressing:

¾ cup (175 g) mayonnaise (we prefer Duke's)
½ cup (112 g) coconut milk
¼ cup (60 g) Thai yellow curry paste
¾ tablespoon white sugar
¼ teaspoon lime juice
¼ teaspoon chicken bouillon powder
¼ teaspoon minced garlic

16 slices potato sandwich bread (we like Martin's)
½ cup (118 g) Curry Boys BBQ Tangy Pickled Cucumbers (page 108)
1 white onion, sliced thinly
1 cup (16 g) chopped cilantro

1. Preheat smoker to 225°F (107°C). Pat chicken dry and lay out on a sheet tray or cutting board. Season chicken liberally on top and bottom with chicken rub. You'll need about 1 teaspoon of rub per chicken thigh. Place chicken onto smoker grates and smoke for 1½ to 2 hours, or until chicken measures at an internal temperature of 165°F (74°C). Remove chicken to cool. Shred the chicken into a large bowl and set aside.
2. Make the dressing: In a medium mixing bowl, whisk together the dressing ingredients.
3. Pour the dressing into the bowl with the shredded chicken. Mix well to make sure everything is evenly coated. Cover and refrigerate for 1 hour for best results.
4. Toast 2 slices of bread per sandwich. On the bottom slice, layer pickle slices, onions, and cilantro. Top with 4 ounces (113 g) of smoked chicken salad. Close sandwich with the other slice of toast. Cut on a diagonal and serve!

Serves 4

SINGHA CAN CHICKEN

Singha is one of Thailand's most popular lagers and a fan favorite at our restaurants. It is light, crisp, refreshing, and works perfectly for our Thai-inspired beer can chicken! This recipe allows the chicken to be smoked to moist perfection with all the smoky-sweet complexity you crave. Once it is finished smoking, you can either carve the whole chicken to enjoy immediately or pull and chop the chicken for other uses. We love saving some for bangin' sandwiches or shredding the chicken for a quick and easy chicken fried rice!

1 (4 to 5 pound [1.8 to 2.3 kg]) whole chicken

For the marinade:

¼ cup (56 g) coconut milk
2 tablespoons (30 ml) fish sauce
2 tablespoons (30 ml) dark soy sauce
2 tablespoons (30 ml) lime juice
1 tablespoon (8 g) grated fresh ginger
2 cloves garlic, minced
1 stalk lemongrass, finely minced
1 Thai chili, finely minced
2 tablespoons (30 ml) vegetable oil

1 can (12 ounces) Thai Singha beer (sub any light lager beer)
1 tablespoon (15 ml) lime juice
1 stalk lemongrass, cut in half
2 cloves garlic, smashed
1-inch (2.5 cm) piece ginger, sliced

For the Thai spice rub:

2 tablespoons (36 g) kosher salt
1 tablespoon (6 g) white pepper
1 tablespoon (12 g) palm sugar or brown sugar
½ tablespoon ground coriander
½ tablespoon ground cumin
1 teaspoon ground turmeric
1 tablespoon (9 g) garlic powder
1 tablespoon (7 g) onion powder
1 teaspoon lemongrass powder
1 teaspoon ground ginger
1 teaspoon Thai red pepper flakes

1. Pat the chicken dry with paper towels.
2. Make the marinade: Mix marinade ingredients in a large bowl and add the chicken. Rub the marinade all over the chicken, including under the skin. Cover the bowl with plastic wrap and marinate in the refrigerator for 4 to 6 hours, or preferably overnight.
3. Open the beer can and pour out (or drink!) about one-half of the beer. Add lime juice, lemongrass, garlic, and ginger to the can.
4. Make the Thai spice rub: Add all of the spice rub ingredients to a small mixing bowl and mix thoroughly.
5. Preheat your smoker to 275°F (135°C). Remove the chicken from the marinade and pat it dry. Coat the chicken evenly with the Thai spice rub. Place the beer can upright in a roasting pan. Carefully lower the chicken onto the beer can so it stands upright. Place the chicken in the smoker, beer can upright, and close the lid. Smoke for 2½ to 3 hours, or until the internal temperature reads 165°F (74°C) in the breast and 175°F (79°C) in the thigh.
6. Carefully remove the chicken from the smoker and let it rest for 15 minutes. Remove the beer can and carve the chicken.

Serves 6

SMOKED DUCK BREAST *FOLD-OVERS*

We first made this dish during a pop-up at one of our favorite restaurants in Nashville called Bad Idea (shout-out to the homie Chef Colby!) and it became an instant classic. There are few things more nostalgic to an American than making a sandwich with white bread. And naturally, when you're an incredible pitmaster like Andrew Samia, you find a way to add a delicious smoked element to make sure that nostalgic bite happens more frequently.

For context, a "foldie" or "fold-over" is a classic pitmaster move that consists of taking a single slice of white bread, topping said piece of bread with a slice of fatty brisket, adding tangy pickles, slathering on a sweet BBQ sauce, and folding the bread over like a taco for a quick two-biter snack. In this version, we use duck breast that is first smoked and then basted with butter, lime juice, and lemongrass over high heat for a more deluxe version of the classic fold-over. It's quiet luxury—kinda like when you blast the AC in your 2014 Toyota Camry, but also purposely decide to roll your windows down. Yeah, that's luxury, baby. —Sean

2 skin-on duck breasts
1 teaspoon kosher salt
1 teaspoon ground white pepper
1 teaspoon Chinese five-spice powder
Pinch white sugar
½ cup (112 g) unsalted butter
2 tablespoons (30 ml) lime juice
1 tablespoon (5 g) finely minced lemongrass
6 slices potato sandwich bread (we like Martin's)
¼ cup (40 g) thinly sliced white onion
¼ cup (36 g) Curry Boys BBQ Tangy Pickled Cucumbers (page 108)
6 tablespoons (128 g) Colby's Famous Thai-Texas Lemongrass BBQ Sauce (page 35)

1. Preheat your smoker to 200°F (93°C). Score the skin on the duck breasts in a crisscross pattern, being careful not to pierce through to the meat. Then, pat the breasts dry with paper towels.
2. Mix together kosher salt, white pepper, Chinese five-spice, and sugar, and then liberally season the duck breasts with the spice mixture. Place the duck breasts in the smoker, skin-side up, as far away from the fire source as possible. Smoke for 40 to 60 minutes or until the internal temperature of each breast reaches 130°F (54°C) for medium-rare. Smoke longer if more doneness is desired. Remove the duck breasts from the smoker and allow them to rest for a few minutes.
3. Add butter to a saucepan or cast-iron skillet over medium-high heat. Once the butter has melted, stir in lime juice and lemongrass and continue to cook until it starts to bubble. When the butter starts bubbling, add the duck breasts to the pan, turn the heat down to low, and baste the duck breasts with the butter mixture for 3 minutes. Remove the duck breasts from the pan and allow to rest for 20 minutes before slicing into ¼-inch (6 mm) slices.
4. Assemble classic Texas fold-overs by topping 1 slice of the potato bread with 3 to 4 slices of duck breast, some thinly sliced white onions, a couple of pickled cucumbers, and a drizzle of lemongrass BBQ sauce. Fold the bread over like a taco and enjoy!

chapter
7

BRISKET AND OTHER BEEF MAINS

COOKING TEXAS-STYLE
BRISKET AT CURRY BOYS BBQ

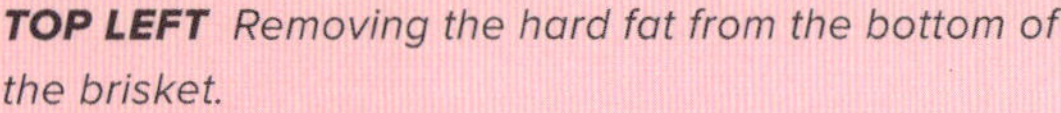

TOP LEFT *Removing the hard fat from the bottom of the brisket.*

TOP MIDDLE *A brisket trimmed and carved to a rounder and more uniform shape.*

TOP RIGHT *Dense wood splits, stacked tightly together on a bed of coals to burn low and slow, are ready for the cook.*

BOTTOM LEFT *Ten hours into the cook, the bark is set and the fat is starting to render, which means it is time to foil-boat the briskets.*

BOTTOM RIGHT *We crimp two sheets of heavy-duty aluminum foil around the brisket, creating a "foil boat."*

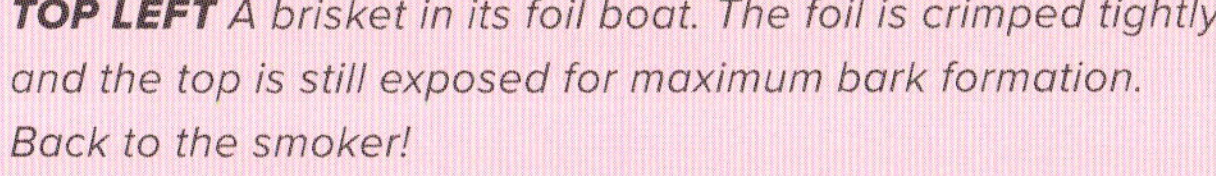

***TOP LEFT** A brisket in its foil boat. The foil is crimped tightly and the top is still exposed for maximum bark formation. Back to the smoker!*

***TOP RIGHT** Two hours later, the brisket is soft and jiggly, and a meat probe slides in like poking warm butter. The brisket is finished and needs to rest before slicing.*

***BOTTOM LEFT** Use a serrated knife to slice the brisket, always against the grain, in ¼-inch (6 mm) slices.*

***BOTTOM RIGHT** A finished and sliced Texas-style beef brisket . . . ready for a bath in some green curry!*

Makes 1 BRISKET

TEXAS-STYLE SMOKED BEEF BRISKET

Texans take their brisket seriously. Like, I mean . . . s e r i o u s l y. Some even consider it gospel. So, it should come as no surprise that our pitmaster Andrew Samia is a frequent attendee at the Church of Brisket—blessing our presence with some of the holiest brisket in all of the land. Brisket, in essence, is easy. It requires only four things: salt, pepper, fire, and time. However, many things can go wrong during the long, 12-hour pilgrimage to reach the holy land of perfectly smoked and seasoned brisket, so it is imperative to follow this recipe with care. Take your time with it, and you will get better with practice. Fire is fickle, and sometimes things just happen. Give yourself some grace and just have fun with it, because let's be real: At the end of the day, it's way more fun to be a sinner than a saint. —Sean

1 whole full packer brisket, ideally prime beef and in the 10 to 12 pound (4.5 to 5.4 kg) range
1 cup (100 g) Curry Boys BBQ Brisket Rub (page 36)

1. In your smoker, build a solid base of burned-down coals to preheat smoker to 250°F (121°C).
2. Start with a full packer brisket. Ideally, we prefer to start with briskets in the 10- to 12-pound (4.5 to 5.4 kg) raw weight range, which will yield approximately 5 to 6 pounds (2.3 to 2.7 kg) after trimming and smoking, enough for 10 to 15 servings. Trim the brisket to your liking. You want to remove the hard fat from the bottom side of the brisket and trim the fat cap on the top of the brisket to about ¼ inch (6 mm). While trimming, the goal is to achieve an even thickness throughout the brisket so that it cooks evenly. You also want to trim off any jagged edges or thin parts that could burn during the cook.
3. We like to moisten the brisket with a spritz of water before seasoning. This will help the seasoning adhere to the brisket. Season the brisket liberally with the brisket rub. Be sure to season every square inch of the brisket, including the edges. After seasoning, carefully pick up the brisket and give it a little shake to remove any excess seasoning. Let rest for 30 minutes while the smoker preheats.

Continued

Continued from previous page

4. Place the brisket in your smoker, fat-side up, and position it as far away from the firebox as possible, with the thicker end facing toward the fire. Smoke for 10 hours. Add post oak wood splits as needed to maintain a smoker temperature of 250°F (121°C). Spritz the edges of the brisket with water occasionally (every hour or so) to knock off ash and cool down the edges that might burn. After 10 hours, the bark on your brisket should be set . . . a good test is to run your finger over the brisket to ensure the seasoning doesn't rub off. If it doesn't rub off, then it's time to foil-boat the brisket.
5. Lay 2 sheets of 18 x 24-inch (46 x 61 cm) heavy-duty aluminum foil on top of each other and place the brisket in the center, fat-side up. Crimp the edges all the way around the brisket, making a "foil boat" for the brisket to rest in, while leaving the top of the brisket exposed. Continue smoking the foil-boated brisket for 2 to 3 hours, until the brisket is soft and jiggly, and a meat probe slides into the thickest part of the flat muscle like poking warm butter. The internal temperature of the finished brisket should be around 200°F to 205°F (93°C to 96°C) when finished.
6. Remove the brisket from the smoker and allow it to rest for at least 30 minutes before slicing, so the juices have time to redistribute throughout the meat. Always slice the brisket against the grain, turning it 90 degrees near the halfway mark where the flat muscle meets the point muscle.

Serves 4

SMOKED BRISKET "THAI" DIP SANDWICH

As a kid, I used to eat at Arby's once a week because my cello teacher's house was close to one. I hated going to cello practice, but I loved Arby's, and my mother knew these things. So, like any good, enterprising mother, she would dangle the proverbial carrot every week to get me to go to cello practice. I, in turn, would end up at Arby's every week—ordering my favorite French dip sandwich. Life was good. I wasn't getting any better at cello, but a love affair for luscious, dipped sandwiches began. Our version of this sandwich takes inspiration from the French dip, but is wholly Thai-inspired. Rather than a rich, beefy au jus, we have an absolutely delicious Thai-Chinese braising sauce that can be found in braised pork belly dishes all over Yaowarat Road in Bangkok. This sandwich is so simple to make, but it packs a flavorful punch because the crusty roll soaks up all of the slightly sweet and savory dipping sauce. And hey, at least I don't have to pick a cello beforehand to eat it. —Sean

For the dipping sauce:

- 5½ tablespoons (66 g) palm sugar or brown sugar
- 4 slices (⅛- to ¼-inch [3 to 6 mm] thick) fresh ginger
- 3 cloves garlic, peeled and smashed
- 2 cups (473 ml) beef stock (sub chicken stock or water)
- 2 tablespoons (30 ml) rice wine
- 3 ounces (89 ml) light or regular soy sauce
- 2 tablespoons (30 ml) fish sauce
- 2 tablespoons (38 g) oyster sauce
- 2 bird's eye chilies, rough-chopped, optional
- 1 cinnamon stick
- 2 star anise
- 1 tablespoon (6 g) ground black pepper

Ingredients continued

1. Make the dipping sauce: Heat up a large wok or saucepan over medium heat. Add sugar and cook until it melts and looks amber in color and is syrupy. Be careful not to burn the sugar. If the sugar burns, clean your pan and start fresh. Add ginger and garlic, stirring to make sure everything is coated, sizzling, and fragrant. Cook and stir occasionally for 2 to 3 minutes. Add the rest of the liquid sauce ingredients and stir to incorporate it all. Make sure the sugar is fully dissolved and incorporated. Bring it to a boil and then add the spices, including chilies if you're looking for an extra kick of spice. Reduce the heat to a gentle simmer. Cover and let the sauce cook until thickened, about 10 to 15 minutes.

Continued

Continued from previous page

For the mayo:

½ cup (113 g) mayonnaise (we prefer Duke's)
1½ tablespoons (23 g) sriracha (adjust to spiciness preference)
1 teaspoon lime juice
¼ teaspoon sesame oil

1½ pounds (680 g) Texas-Style Smoked Beef Brisket (can use leftovers), hot, sliced ¼-inch (6 mm) thick (page 157)
4 medium kaiser rolls or crusty bread of choice
1½ tablespoons (21 g) unsalted butter
8 slices provolone cheese

2. Make the mayo: In a small bowl, mix together mayo ingredients until the mixture is smooth and creamy.
3. Preheat oven to high broil. Slice rolls in half. Lightly butter the tops of the rolls. Spread mayo on bottom half of the roll and then place ¼ to ⅓ pound (113 to 150 g) of sliced brisket on top of the mayo. Place 2 slices of provolone cheese on top of the brisket—covering as much of the brisket as possible. Broil for a few minutes, just until the cheese is properly melted and the buttered tops of the rolls are golden brown. Serve the sandwiches with the dipping sauce, and happy dipping!

Serves 4

THAI-STYLE SMOKED BRISKET FRIED RICE

Fried rice is ubiquitous in Asian cuisine. I mean, we're almost positive every East Asian and Southeast Asian country has their own version of fried rice. Why? It's the perfect "clean-out-your-fridge" meal that is affordable, easy to make, and always delicious. It's Asian soul food. When compared to the popular Chinese-style fried rice, Thai-style fried rice is typically punchier and bolder in flavor due to the savory fish sauce and sweet oyster sauce. We love serving it with a side of Thailand's favorite sauce: prik nam pla. We also garnish it with a lime wedge—a nice squeeze of citrus complements the rich brisket beautifully.

For the sauce:

2 tablespoons (30 ml) soy sauce
2 tablespoons (30 ml) fish sauce
1 tablespoon (19 g) oyster sauce
1 teaspoon ground white pepper
1 teaspoon palm sugar or brown sugar

4 cups (660 g) cooked jasmine rice (cold, day-old rice works best)
5 tablespoons (75 ml) vegetable oil (sub brisket fat, if you have it), divided
6 cloves garlic, minced
⅓ cup (37 g) small-diced carrots
1 pound (454 g) Texas-Style Smoked Beef Brisket, hot, chopped into small bite-size pieces (page 157)
4 eggs, beaten
½ cup (24 g) chopped green onions
½ cup (80 g) sliced white onion
2 cucumbers, sliced
12 fresh lime wedges
½ cup (8 g) chopped cilantro
4 small dishes Prik Nam Pla (page 51)

1. Make the sauce: In a small mixing bowl, combine sauce ingredients. Set aside.
2. Break rice apart so that it is not clumpy. This prepares it for stir-frying. Use your hands or 2 forks. Set aside.
3. Heat 3 tablespoons (45 ml) of vegetable oil in a large pan or wok over medium heat. Add garlic and sauté for 30 seconds. (Make sure not to burn!) Add carrots and chopped brisket and stir-fry for 2 minutes. Slide carrots and brisket to one side of the wok to make room to scramble the eggs.
4. Pour beaten eggs on the empty side of the pan and scramble for 1 to 1½ minutes. Turn heat to high and add the remaining 2 tablespoons (30 ml) of vegetable oil to the pan. Add day-old jasmine rice and stir-fry everything together well. Make sure to scrape the bottom and sides of the pan to ensure everything is mixed together.
5. Add sauce mixture evenly over rice, making sure everything is coated. Stir-fry evenly for 3 minutes. Mix in green onions and white onions and continue cooking and mixing for another 2 to 3 minutes.
6. Divide fried rice onto 4 plates and garnish with sliced cucumber, fresh lime wedges, chopped cilantro, and a side of prik nam pla sauce!

Serves **4 TO 6**

VIETNAMESE SHAKING BEEF *with* **SMOKED BRISKET**

Bò lúc lắc, a Vietnamese dish, gets a wild makeover with smoked brisket. Imagine smoky, melt-in-your-mouth brisket mixed with classic stir-fried flavors—it's a seriously satisfying and delicious meal, perfect for a fancy party or a casual hangout with friends. The brisket is smoked low and slow and absorbs the amazing flavor of post oak smoke. Then, it's cut into big chunks and seared to create a crispy outside while keeping the inside tender. Toss these tasty pieces in a tangy lime and pepper sauce, and you get a perfect mix of rich meat and bright, refreshing flavors. Like any good dish, we recommend serving it with a side of white rice so that it soaks up the delicious sauce. Top it all off with fresh herbs and scallions for an extra boost of flavor.

2 tablespoons (30 ml) soy sauce
1 tablespoon (19 g) oyster sauce
1 tablespoon (15 ml) fish sauce
1 tablespoon (30 ml) lime juice
1 tablespoon (15 g) brown sugar
2 cloves garlic, minced
1 teaspoon ground black pepper
1½ pounds (680 g) Texas-Style Smoked Beef Brisket, cold, cut into 1-inch (2.5 cm) cubes (page 157)
2 tablespoons (30 ml) vegetable oil
2 tablespoons (28 g) unsalted butter
1 red bell pepper, sliced into chunks
1 red onion, sliced into wedges
1 tablespoon (15 ml) rice vinegar

For the dipping sauce:

2 teaspoons salt
1 teaspoon ground black pepper
2 tablespoons (30 ml) fresh lime juice

1 tomato, sliced
1 cucumber, sliced into rounds
½ cup (8 g) chopped cilantro
2 tablespoons (6 g) chopped green onion

1. In a large mixing bowl, combine and mix soy sauce, oyster sauce, fish sauce, lime juice, brown sugar, garlic, and black pepper. Mix well. Add smoked brisket cubes and mix well, making sure everything is evenly coated. Set aside for 5 to 10 minutes.
2. In a large pan or wok, heat vegetable oil on medium to high heat. Add in brisket cubes, making sure each piece is getting a sear. Cook for about 1½ minutes per side, then flip and cook for another 1½ minutes on the other side. Shake the pan so the brisket sears evenly and gets a nice crisp.
3. Push the brisket cubes to one side of the pan. Add in and melt the butter on the empty side of the pan. Add in bell pepper and red onion to cook, and continue shaking the pan to make sure everything is getting coated and cooking evenly, about 2 to 3 minutes. Slowly add in rice vinegar while stirring to mix everything.
4. Make the dipping sauce: In a small sauce dish or plate, combine the dipping sauce ingredients.
5. Line the edge of a large serving platter with sliced tomatoes and cucumber. Neatly plate the shaking beef in the center. Garnish with chopped cilantro and green onions and serve with dipping sauce on the side! Goes great with jasmine rice.

NOTE:
The brisket should be made the day before. This recipe calls for cold brisket.

Serves 8

SMOKED BRISKET *and* THAI GREEN CURRY *with* ROASTED CAULIFLOWER

A wise person once said, "Perfection is achieved, not when there is nothing more to add, but when there is nothing left to take away." Now, we couldn't tell you who said this, but gosh darn, this dish is as close to perfect as possible. In fact, this is the dish that started it all for us. No, really. Like, without this dish, there is no Curry Boys. Inspired by a brisket burnt-end dish from Eem—one of our favorite restaurants in America (shout-out to Eric and Chef Earl)—we pair an aromatic and herbaceous green curry to cut through a rich, fatty slice of Texas-style smoked brisket. When eaten with a spoonful of rice, it's simple perfection. There's a reason why this will always be our restaurant's most popular dish!

2 tablespoons (30 ml) vegetable oil
1 tablespoon (15 ml) fish sauce
½ teaspoon garlic powder
½ teaspoon salt
1 tablespoon (15 ml) lime juice
1 large head of cauliflower, cut into florets
2¼ quarts (2.1 L) Thai Green Curry Sauce (page 25)
8 servings Thai jasmine rice
3 pounds (1.4 kg) Texas-Style Smoked Beef Brisket, hot, sliced into ¼-inch (6 mm) slices (page 157)
¼ cup (40 g) fried shallots
¼ cup (4 g) chopped cilantro
¼ cup (10 g) chopped Thai basil
Crispy Garlic Chili Oil (page 45), optional
Curry Boys BBQ Tangy Pickled Cucumbers (page 108), optional

1. Preheat oven to 425°F (218°C). Line a baking sheet with parchment paper.
2. In a large mixing bowl, combine and mix vegetable oil, fish sauce, garlic powder, salt, and lime juice. Add in cauliflower florets and mix well, making sure cauliflower is evenly coated with the seasonings. Spread cauliflower florets out on the baking sheet so they are not touching. Roast for 20 to 25 minutes, flipping halfway through, until cauliflower is golden brown.
3. Add Thai green curry sauce to a large pot over medium to high heat. Add in roasted cauliflower while stirring and bring curry to a low simmer. Curry is ready.
4. To serve, scoop a portion of jasmine rice into one side of a bowl. Pour one ladle of green curry and cauliflower onto the empty side of the bowl. Add 2 to 3 slices of brisket on top of the green curry and cauliflower, and then ladle extra curry broth over the brisket. Garnish with fried shallots, chopped cilantro, and Thai basil. Serve with chili oil and house pickles if you're wanting an extra flavor bomb!

PRO TIP:
If you want to make a vegan version of this tasty cauliflower curry, substitute soy sauce for the fish sauce and omit the chicken bouillon powder.

Serves 4

SMOKED BRISKET *LETTUCE WRAPS*

Anyone who says that a lettuce-wrapped version of brisket isn't worth the time and the hassle is just plain wrong! Lettuce can be scary . . . and green . . . and leafy. But that's okay, people! Lettuce can also be the perfect vehicle for a beautifully smoked salty, peppery Texas smoked brisket. Now, if you don't want the hassle of smoking a brisket just for this recipe, then at least consider this recipe when you have leftover brisket. There is a subtle depth and complexity with the nam jim jaew sauce, followed by an olfactory punch from some fresh herbs—every bite possibly more refreshing than the last.

2 tablespoons (30 ml) fish sauce
1 tablespoon (15 ml) soy sauce
1 tablespoon (15 ml) lime juice
1 tablespoon (15 g) brown sugar
1 clove garlic, minced
1 teaspoon Thai chili flakes (adjust to spiciness preference)
2 pounds (907 g) Texas-Style Smoked Beef Brisket (can use leftovers), chopped until shredded (page 157)
1 large head lettuce, separated into leaves
½ cup (20 g) chopped Thai basil
½ cup (8 g) chopped cilantro
½ cup (48 g) chopped mint
1 cup (119 g) thinly sliced cucumbers
1 cup (236 g) Vietnamese-Style "Đồ Chua" Pickled Carrot and Daikon (page 104)
1¼ cups (296 ml) Nam Jim Jaew (page 52)
½ cup (80 g) fried shallots
2 tablespoons (30 ml) Crispy Garlic Chili Oil (page 45)

1. In a large pan on medium heat, combine fish sauce, soy sauce, lime juice, brown sugar, garlic, and chili flakes. Stir and mix well until combined. Add in chopped brisket. Stir to make sure everything is coated evenly. Cook brisket until it is warm to hot and there is caramelization happening.
2. On a large platter, neatly place lettuce cups, Thai basil, cilantro, mint, cucumbers, and pickled carrot and daikon on one side. On the opposite side of the platter, use tongs to neatly plate chopped brisket. Serve with small sauce dishes of nam jim jaew. To assemble wraps, put brisket inside a lettuce cup and top with fresh herbs, pickles, fried shallots, and chili crisp. Dip or pour sauce on for the perfect bite!

THAI RED CURRY–SPICED SMOKED PRIME RIB

Prime rib: It's basically the Beyoncé (shout out Texas!) of all beef cuts, and this recipe is the spicy, saucy, show-stopping number that'll make anyone crazy in love. *We're taking that* flawless *hunk of marbled goodness and giving it a red curry–coated smoke bath before it gets into* formation *on the grill for a sexy reverse sear. This recipe is absolutely* irreplaceable *and will be a guaranteed knockout for any dinner party, Friendsgiving, bachelor party, or even a gathering of* single ladies.

1 (5 to 6 pound [2.3 to 2.7 kg]) bone-in prime rib roast (1 bone for every 2 guests)
2 tablespoons (36 g) kosher salt, plus more as needed

For the spice rub:

1 tablespoon (6 g) 16-mesh black pepper
1 tablespoon (12 g) palm sugar or brown sugar
2 tablespoons (30 g) Thai red curry paste
1 tablespoon (15 ml) fish sauce
1 tablespoon (15 ml) dark soy sauce
2 tablespoons (30 ml) lime juice
1 tablespoon (5 g) finely minced lemongrass
1 tablespoon (8 g) grated fresh ginger
3 cloves garlic, minced
1 tablespoon (6 g) ground coriander
1 teaspoon ground cumin
1 teaspoon turmeric powder
1 teaspoon red pepper flakes
2 tablespoons (30 ml) olive oil

½ cup (112 g) unsalted butter
¼ cup (56 g) coconut milk
1 tablespoon (2 g) lime zest
1 tablespoon (1 g) chopped cilantro
1 teaspoon chopped Thai basil

1. Pat the prime rib dry with paper towels. Season all sides of the prime rib with 2 tablespoons (36 g) of kosher salt.
2. Make the spice rub: Add rub ingredients to a small mixing bowl and mix well to combine.
3. Using your hands, rub the spice mixture all over the prime rib to get it completely coated, then wrap the prime rib in plastic wrap and refrigerate overnight.
4. The next day, take the prime rib out of the refrigerator, scrape off any pockets of excess rub, and allow meat to rest on the counter while your smoker preheats to 225°F (107°C).
5. Give the prime rib one last sprinkle of kosher salt and place prime rib bone-side down in the smoker, as far away from the fire source as possible, and smoke at 225°F (107°C) for 45 minutes.
6. Meanwhile, melt butter in a small saucepan over medium-low heat. Add coconut milk, lime zest, cilantro, and Thai basil. Whisk to combine. Bring to a light simmer, then remove from heat and set aside.
7. After the prime rib has smoked for 45 minutes, use a silicone brush to baste the prime rib with the butter mixture. Continue to smoke at 225°F (107°C) while basting the prime rib every 45 minutes for approximately 3 to 4 hours or until the internal temperature of the prime rib reaches 130°F (54°C) for medium-rare. Remove the prime rib from the smoker and let it rest while you prepare your grill for a high-heat reverse sear.
8. Prepare your grill for high heat by building a high bed of burned-down wood or lump charcoal. Give the prime rib one last baste with the butter mixture, then sear it directly over the coals for 2 minutes per side to develop a good crust. Remove the prime rib from the grill and allow it to rest for 20 to 30 minutes before slicing.

Makes 2 TO 2½ POUNDS (0.9 TO 1.1 KG)

SMOKED BEEF CHEEK BARBACOA

There's nothing quite like a Sunday morning in Texas, where the only real question is: "Where's the barbacoa?" Seriously, it's practically a ritual. You roll out of bed, maybe a little groggy, and suddenly, the rich, smoky aroma of slow-cooked beef cheek barbacoa fills the air. It's a dish with deep roots in Tex-Mex culture—a celebration of flavors and community that brings friends and family together over breakfast tacos and good vibes.

Now, we like to switch things up a bit. Our recipe takes that traditional barbacoa and gives it a Thai twist that you wouldn't expect, but will absolutely adore. Here's the kicker: We throw in some fish sauce and tamarind paste, which cut through the rich fattiness of the beef cheek and add a punch of umami that's out of this world. Trust me, your taste buds and your tortilla will thank you.

- 4 pounds (1.8 kg) trimmed beef cheeks (5 to 6 beef cheeks)
- ¼ cup (18 g) finely chopped lemongrass
- 6 cloves garlic, finely minced
- 2 shallots, finely minced
- ¼ cup (60 ml) fish sauce
- 2 tablespoons (30 ml) dark soy sauce
- 2 tablespoons (24 g) palm sugar or brown sugar
- 1 tablespoon (15 g) tamarind paste
- 2 Thai chilies, finely minced
- 1 tablespoon (15 ml) vegetable oil
- ½ cup (118 ml) beef broth

1. Pat dry the beef cheeks with paper towels. Make sure to trim off any silver skin or excess fat if the beef cheeks did not come pretrimmed. In a blender, add the rest of the ingredients except the beef broth; blend until smooth. Place trimmed beef cheeks in a medium mixing bowl and pour the blended marinade over the meat, ensuring everything is evenly coated. Cover and refrigerate overnight.
2. The next day, preheat your smoker to 250°F (121°C). Remove the beef cheeks from the marinade and place them directly on the smoker grates, as far away from the fire source as possible. Reserve the marinade. Smoke the beef cheeks at 250°F (121°C) for 4 hours to develop a good bark.
3. In the meantime, pour the marinade into a small saucepan over high heat. Bring to a rolling boil for 10 minutes to kill any harmful bacteria. Turn off the heat and reserve the marinade for later in the recipe.
4. At the 4-hour mark, transfer the beef cheeks to a foil pan, add the beef broth and the reserved marinade to the bottom of the pan, and cover the pan tightly with aluminum foil. Place the foil-wrapped pan in the smoker and continue smoking at 250°F (121°C) for 2 to 3 more hours, or until the beef cheeks reach an internal temperature of 203°F (95°C) and a meat probe thermometer slides in and out with no resistance, like poking warm butter.
5. Once the beef cheeks have finished smoking, remove the pan and allow them to rest for 20 minutes. Remove the beef cheeks from the pan and, using either forks or your hands, shred the meat. Skim off any excess fat from the liquid left in the smoking pan, and then add the shredded meat to the pan liquid and mix well. Works great in fried rice and stir-fries, such as our version of Pad See Ew on page 175!

PRO TIP:

This smoked barbacoa works great in a flour tortilla, with fried rice, or added to a stir-fry!

ORDER
HERE

DRAFT BEER
>Pinthouse Electric Jellyfish Hazy IPA 8.95
>Yellow Rose IPA 8.95
>Lone Star 4.95
>Lovestruck Hefe 7.50
>Betty Kolsch 7.50
>Sapporo 6.75
>Modelo Especial 5.95
Lone Pint
Brewery

Smokeout
PASSION FRUIT
SAKE SLUSH
Kid Super
Curry Boys BBQ
CURRY BOYS BBQ
New!

Serves 4

PAD SEE EW WITH SMOKED BEEF CHEEK BARBACOA

Some people are Team Pad Thai, and some people are Team Pad See Ew. It's one of those great debates that will probably never be settled—like Team Edward versus Team Jacob. If you don't understand that reference, it's probably because you've got way better things to do than to speed-read through the entire Twilight *series. All we know is, the smokiness and saltiness of the beef cheek and the sweetness of the pad see ew sauce in this recipe create a flavor combo more enchanting than when Edward first smelled Bella. If you don't understand that reference, it's probably because . . . just read* Twilight*, please. And then make this delicious pad see ew recipe.*

1 pound (454 g) Smoked Beef Cheek Barbacoa, cold, shredded (page 172)
1 tablespoon + ¼ cup (15 ml + 60 ml) vegetable oil, divided

For the sauce:

3 tablespoons (45 ml) light soy sauce
1½ tablespoons (22 ml) dark soy sauce
1½ tablespoons (29 g) oyster sauce
2 teaspoons palm sugar or brown sugar
¾ teaspoon white pepper

1 cup (71 g) broccoli florets
1 cup (110 g) shredded or julienned carrots
6 cloves garlic, minced
4 eggs, beaten
4 servings cooked wide rice noodles
8 lime wedges
¼ cup (4 g) chopped cilantro
1 bunch green onion, dark green ends, chopped
Thai chili powder or flakes

1. In a large pan, heat 1 tablespoon (15 ml) of vegetable oil on medium to high heat. Add the cold, shredded barbacoa and cook until barbacoa is a bit crispy, 3 to 4 minutes. Remove from pan to a large bowl or plate and set to the side.
2. Make the sauce: In a small mixing bowl, combine all sauce ingredients and set to the side.
3. In a large wok or pan, heat 1 tablespoon (15 ml) of vegetable oil on medium to high heat. Add in broccoli and carrots and cook for 3 to 4 minutes. Remove from pan to the barbacoa bowl.
4. Add the remaining 3 tablespoons (45 ml) of vegetable oil to the pan, then add garlic and sauté for 30 seconds. Make sure not to burn! Slide garlic to one side of the wok. Pour in eggs and scramble them on the empty side of the pan.
5. Add cooked rice noodles to pan and mix everything together well. Add sauce mixture evenly over noodles, making sure everything is coated. Cook evenly for 2 minutes. Mix in crispy smoked barbacoa, broccoli, and carrots, and continue mixing and cooking for another 2 to 3 minutes.
6. Divide onto 4 plates and garnish with lime wedges, chopped cilantro, green onions, and Thai chili flakes!

NOTE:
The barbacoa should be made the day before. This recipe calls for cold barbacoa.

Serves 4

SPICE-RUBBED SMOKED BEEF *SHORT RIBS*

Yabba dabba dooooo! These are your classic, Fred Flintstone–approved, Texas smoked beef ribs, but we've amped up the flavor drastically by glazing them with coconut milk, fish sauce, honey, and lime juice. We highly recommend squeezing some fresh lime juice on the ribs before taking a bite for a little extra acidity to cut through the richness of the super marbled beef!

1 rack beef chuck short ribs, bone-in (3 to 4 pounds [1.4 to 1.8 kg])

For the rub:

2 tablespoons (36 g) kosher salt
1 tablespoon (6 g) 16-mesh black pepper
1 tablespoon (12 g) palm sugar or brown sugar
2 teaspoons ground coriander
2 teaspoons ground cumin
1 teaspoon ground turmeric
1 teaspoon ground star anise
1 tablespoon (9 g) lemongrass powder
1 tablespoon (9 g) garlic powder
1 tablespoon (7 g) onion powder

For the mop sauce:

¼ cup (56 g) coconut milk
2 tablespoons (30 ml) fish sauce
2 tablespoons (30 ml) dark soy sauce
2 tablespoons (40 g) honey
1 tablespoon (15 ml) lime juice
1 teaspoon grated ginger
1 clove garlic, minced

½ cup (8 g) chopped cilantro
2 limes, cut into 8 wedges
1 tablespoon (3 g) toasted sesame seeds

1. Pat the rack of beef ribs dry with paper towels. Trim any thick pockets of fat, leaving just a thin layer.
2. Make the rub: Add rub ingredients to a small mixing bowl and mix until well combined.
3. Liberally season the rack of beef ribs with the spice rub, ensuring that all sides are well-coated. Refrigerate the rack of ribs overnight before smoking for deeper spice penetration.
4. The next day, remove the ribs from the refrigerator and allow them to rest on the counter while you preheat your smoker to 250°F (121°C).
5. Place the ribs in the smoker, bone-side down, as far away from the fire source as possible. Smoke at 250°F (121°C) for 5 hours.
6. Make the mop sauce: Meanwhile, prepare mop sauce by combining ingredients in a small mixing bowl and whisking them together until fully incorporated.
7. After 5 hours, your ribs should have developed a good bark, and you can start to mop them. Using a silicone brush or BBQ mop, mop the rack of ribs with coconut milk mixture every 20 minutes until the ribs are finished smoking, approximately 2 more hours. The ribs are finished when they reach an internal temperature of 203°F (95°C) and a meat probe thermometer slides in and out with little to no resistance, like poking warm butter. Remove the ribs from the smoker, give them one final mop with the coconut milk mixture, and wrap them in foil to rest for at least 30 minutes before slicing.
8. Slice the rack into individual bones and arrange on a platter. Garnish with chopped cilantro, lime wedges, and toasted sesame seeds.

Serves 4

WOOD-GRILLED RIB EYE *with* THAI SMASHED POTATOES *and Prik Nam Pla*

This is Andrew Samia's "death row" meal. He would eat this every single day if his wife let him—but like most significant others, her logic prevails. Andrew probably shouldn't be consuming that much saturated fat due to his semi-high cholesterol, although he might argue that this rib eye recipe is so good that he'd sacrifice his health for it. What honestly sets this steak recipe apart from others is the introduction of the prik nam pla sauce that plays perfectly with the smoky, charred steak. It's impossibly good. —Sean

¼ cup (60 ml) vegetable oil, divided

2 rib eye steaks, 1½ inches (3.8 cm) thick, ideally prime beef about 2 to 2½ pounds (0.9 to 1.1 kg) total

2 tablespoons (36 g) kosher salt, divided, plus more as needed

2 pounds (907 g) small Yukon gold potatoes

For the potato sauce:

2 tablespoons (30 ml) fish sauce

2 tablespoons (30 ml) lime juice

2 tablespoons (30 ml) rice vinegar

1 tablespoon (9 g) minced Thai red chili

1 teaspoon light soy sauce

1 teaspoon white sugar

1 clove garlic, minced

½ cup (112 g) unsalted butter, melted

⅓ cup (5 g) roughly chopped cilantro

¼ cup (12 g) thinly sliced green onions

Ingredients continued

1. Preheat oven to 450°F (232°C) and lightly coat a sheet pan with 1 tablespoon (15 ml) of vegetable oil. Preheat your smoker to 225°F (107°C). Remove the rib eyes from the fridge and let them rest on the counter for 15 to 30 minutes. Pat the steaks dry with paper towels to remove excess moisture. Liberally season the steaks with the remaining 1 tablespoon (18 g) of kosher salt, ensuring that the sides are also well-seasoned.
2. Place the steaks in the smoker, positioning them as far away from the fire as possible. Smoke at 225°F (107°C) until the internal temperature of the rib eyes reaches 120°F (49°C), about 1 hour. Remove from the smoker to briefly rest.
3. While the steaks are smoking, prepare your grill for high heat by building a high bed of burned-down wood or lump charcoal. Place a cast-iron pan on the grill grates, directly over the bed of coals, and allow it to get ripping hot. The pan will start to smoke when it is ready.
4. Place potatoes in a large pot and cover them with enough cold water to completely submerge them. Add 1 tablespoon (18 g) of kosher salt and bring to a boil over high heat. Reduce the heat to medium-low and simmer potatoes, uncovered, for about 15 minutes, or until they are tender enough to be pierced with a fork. Strain potatoes with a colander.
5. Make the potato sauce: While potatoes are simmering, prepare your sauce. Add all sauce ingredients except cilantro and green onions to a small mixing bowl. Whisk to combine and dissolve the sugar. Then fold in the cilantro and green onions.

Continued

Continued from previous page

1 cup (235 ml) Prik Nam Pla (page 51)
Flake sea salt
½ cup (20 g) whole leaves Thai basil
½ cup (8 g) whole leaves cilantro

6. Spread strained potatoes on the baking sheet in a single layer. Using the bottom of a glass cup, smash each potato until they are roughly ½-inch (13 mm) thick. Pour the remaining 3 tablespoons (45 ml) of vegetable oil over potatoes and gently mix to ensure both sides are coated evenly. Season to taste with kosher salt, and roast in the oven at 450°F (232°C) for 40 minutes, or until crispy and golden brown. Transfer potatoes to a serving platter and drizzle the prepared sauce over the top.
7. Sear steaks for approximately 1 minute on each side, and 30 seconds on each edge. This should bring the internal temperature of the steaks to 135°F (57°C) for medium-rare. Remove the steaks from the pan to a cutting board and allow them to rest for 15 minutes before slicing.
8. Put 2 to 3 smashed potatoes on each plate. Slice the 2 rib eye steaks against the grain, then divide the sliced steak evenly between the 4 plates. Garnish the steaks with a sprinkle of flake sea salt, some Thai basil, and whole leaf cilantro. Serve with a ramekin of prik nam pla for dipping or spooning over the steak.

Serves 4

Smoked and Grilled CHEESEBURGERS *with* THAI CHILI BACON JAM

Look, we get it. Smash burgers are all the rage these days. We're not hating, but sometimes we just want to eat a thick, juicy burger. This elevated burger features a meticulous process for absolutely maximum flavor and texture. It's gently smoked, rested in warm beef fat to retain moisture and richness, and finished with a fiery char. Crisp lettuce and acidic pickles provide contrasting freshness, but the key ingredient is our sweet, savory, and spicy Thai chili bacon jam. The result is a culinary symphony seemingly conducted by Leonard Bernstein himself!

½ cup (115 g) mayonnaise (we like Duke's)
1 tablespoon (15 g) sriracha
1 teaspoon lime juice
1 teaspoon fish sauce

For the Thai chili bacon jam:

1 pound (454 g) thick-cut bacon, diced
1 shallot, thinly sliced
3 cloves garlic, minced
4 Thai chilies, finely minced
1 teaspoon nam prik pao (Thai chili paste; we prefer Maepranom)
2 tablespoons (30 ml) fish sauce
1 tablespoon (15 ml) lime juice
1 teaspoon white sugar
¼ cup (48 g) palm sugar or brown sugar
1 tablespoon (15 ml) rice vinegar
2 teaspoons soy sauce

Ingredients continued

1. Mix mayonnaise, sriracha, lime juice, and fish sauce in a small bowl. Cover and refrigerate.
2. Make the Thai chili bacon jam: Add diced bacon to a pan and sauté over medium heat until browned and crisp. Remove bacon with a slotted spoon. Add sliced shallot and minced garlic to the pan with the rendered bacon fat and cook for a few minutes until softened. Then, add minced Thai chili and nam prik pao and sauté for an additional 2 minutes. Put bacon back in the pan with the garlic mixture, and then add the rest of the bacon jam ingredients. Stir mixture well to incorporate fully, then simmer for 15 minutes, until it has reduced to a jamlike consistency. Transfer the Thai chili bacon jam to a container and set aside.

Continued

Continued from previous page

- 2 pounds (907 g) fresh 80/20 ground beef
- 1 tablespoon (18 g) kosher salt
- 2 teaspoons ground black pepper
- 1 quart (946 ml) beef tallow, melted
- 8 slices Muenster cheese
- 4 brioche hamburger buns
- ¼ cup (56 g) unsalted butter, softened
- Bibb lettuce
- ¼ cup (36 g) Curry Boys BBQ Tangy Pickled Cucumbers (page 108)

3. Preheat your smoker to 225°F (107°C). Prepare a shallow pan filled with the melted beef tallow.
4. Divide ground beef into 4 burger patties. Be gentle when forming the patties, as over-compacting or overworking the meat will result in a dense, tough burger. Season both sides of each burger with kosher salt and black pepper.
5. Smoke the burgers in the smoker for about 45 minutes. The goal here is not to cook the burgers all the way through, but just to infuse them with the smoke. You should aim to achieve an internal temperature of approximately 115°F (46°C) during this step.
6. After the burgers have smoked, remove them from the smoker and submerge them in the melted beef tallow. Let the burger patties rest in the melted tallow for 30 minutes to absorb the extra-rich beefy flavor.
7. While the burgers are resting, prepare your grill for high heat by building a high bed of burned-down wood or lump charcoal. Remove the burgers from the tallow and grill them directly on the grate over the hot coals for 2 minutes per side, allowing them to achieve an excellent charred finish and your desired level of doneness. Top each patty with 2 slices of cheese during the last minute of grilling to melt the cheese. Remove the patties from the grill and rest on a wire rack before assembling the burgers.
8. Toast the brioche buns in a pan over medium heat with butter until golden brown.
9. Brush both the top and bottom of each bun with the sriracha mayo and then assemble the burgers in the following manner: bottom bun, bibb lettuce, 4 slices of pickled cucumbers, smoked cheeseburger patty, and a generous spoonful of the Thai chili bacon jam. Finish with the top bun and enjoy!

chapter
8

PORK AND LAMB MAINS

Makes 5½ POUNDS (2.5 KG)

SMOKED *and* PULLED PORK

Let's talk about pulled pork, shall we? This dish is the definition of juicy, melt-in-your-mouth goodness, and honestly, it's a BBQ staple for a reason. There's something about that low-and-slow cooking process that transforms a humble piece of pork into a glorious work of shredded art.

Pulled pork has earned its place in the barbecue world because it loves to soak up flavors like nobody's business. You can slather it with your favorite lemongrass BBQ sauce, have it submerged in a creamy Penang curry, or simply enjoy it plain, letting that smoky, sweet, and savory taste shine through. In either case, it's ridiculously delicious. And we're proud of ourselves for making absolutely zero "butt" jokes.

1 bone-in pork butt, around 9 pounds (4.1 kg)
1 cup (100 g) Curry Boys BBQ Pork Rub (page 38), plus more as needed

1. In your smoker, build a solid base of burned-down coals. Preheat to 250°F (121°C).
2. Pat dry the pork butt with paper towels. Liberally season the pork with the rub, making sure to season all sides and edges.
3. Put the pork butt in your smoker, fat-side up, as far away from the firebox as possible. Smoke for 10 hours, adding post oak wood splits as needed to maintain your smoker temperature at 250°F (121°C). Spritz the edges of the pork butt with water occasionally (every hour or so) to knock off ash and also cool down the edges that might burn.
4. At the 10-hour mark, it's time to wrap your pork butt. Lay down 2 sheets of 24 x 24-inch (61 x 61 cm) heavy-duty foil on top of each other and place the pork butt in the center. Fold the sides of the foil up over the top to completely wrap the pork butt in the foil. Be careful not to puncture the foil with the bone from the pork butt, which can sometimes be visible this far into the cook.
5. Return the foil wrapped pork butt to the smoker and continue smoking for roughly 2 more hours. The pork butt is done cooking when a meat thermometer probe slides in and out with little to no resistance, like poking warm butter. The internal temperature should be around 200°F (93°C). Remove the pork butt from the smoker and allow it to rest for 30 minutes.
6. After the pork butt has rested, remove it from the foil and place the pork in a pan or baking dish. Remove the bone, and then pull the meat into strands using your hands. At this point, it's ready to serve, but you can also sprinkle a little more pork BBQ rub on the pulled pork for an extra flavor boost!

Serves 4

BÚN THỊT NƯỚNG *with* SMOKED *and* SEARED PULLED PORK

Bún thịt nướng is another incredible example of why Southeast Asian food is perfect: crunchy pickled veggies, sweet glazed meat, funky nước chấm dressing, pillowy white rice, and all adorned with fresh, aromatic herbs. Chef's kiss. Traditionally, bún thịt nướng is served with thinly sliced grilled pork; slightly sweet, slightly charred. In our "leftover edition" iteration of this dish, we still get char from using smoked, then seared, pulled pork, and the sweet glaze we have provides a slightly sweet touch.

¼ cups (59 ml) lemon-lime soda
2½ tablespoons (48 g) oyster sauce
2 tablespoons (30 g) brown sugar
1½ tablespoons (7 g) finely minced lemongrass
2 teaspoons garlic, finely minced
½ teaspoon paprika
1 pound (454 g) Smoked and Pulled Pork (page 187), warm or room temperature, chopped
1 tablespoon (15 ml) vegetable oil
8 ounces (227 g) rice vermicelli noodles (look for a Vietnamese brand)
1 cup (75 g) shredded lettuce
1 cucumber, sliced
¼ cup (4 g) chopped cilantro
¼ cup (24 g) chopped mint
¼ cup (10 g) chopped Thai basil
¾ cup (177 g) Vietnamese-Style "Đồ Chua" Pickled Carrot and Daikon (page 104)
¼ cup (35 g) crushed roasted peanuts
1¼ cups (285 ml) Nước Chấm (page 49)
Sriracha, optional

1. In a large mixing bowl, combine soda, oyster sauce, brown sugar, lemongrass, garlic, and paprika. Mix well. Stir in chopped pulled pork and combine thoroughly.
2. Heat vegetable oil in a large pan over medium heat to high heat. Add pork mixture to pan. Spread out to sear evenly. Cook until pulled pork is a little crispy and sauce is caramelized, about 3 minutes. Remove from heat and set aside.
3. In a medium pot, bring 3 quarts (2.8 L) of water to a boil and add noodles (check noodle package for instructions). Noodles should be done usually within 4 to 7 minutes. Drain noodles and run under cold water. Divide cooked noodles into 4 bowls.
4. On the outside edges of the bowls, add lettuce, cucumber, cilantro, mint, basil, and pickles. Add a healthy amount of crispy smoked and glazed pulled pork in the center. Garnish with crushed peanuts over the bowl, and serve with a side of nước chấm dipping sauce. For extra spiciness, add some sriracha over the bowls! Mix well and enjoy.

KING OF THE CURRY

Serves 8

SMOKED PULLED PORK THAI PENANG CURRY *with* BROCCOLI *and* YELLOW PEPPERS

When we were coming up with this dish, we contemplated initially pairing the pulled pork with a different curry, but we just couldn't shake the fact that pork and Penang curry go together like peanut butter and jelly. In fact, we hope in the very near future, people start using the very alliterative idiom "goes together like Penang and pulled pork" instead of "peanut butter and jelly." We can dream, right? One of the reasons why this combination works so well is that pulled pork does such an amazing job of trapping the curry in all of its nooks and crannies, so every bite is always flavor-packed with Penang curry.

3 tablespoons (45 ml) vegetable oil
2 teaspoons soy sauce
1 teaspoon turmeric powder
1 teaspoon garlic powder
1 teaspoon lime juice
1 teaspoon palm sugar or brown sugar
½ teaspoon white pepper
½ teaspoon chili flakes or powder (adjust to your spiciness preference)
4 cups (284 g) broccoli heads, cut into florets
2 yellow bell peppers, sliced
2¼ quarts (2.1 L) Thai Penang Curry Sauce (page 28)
3 pounds (1.4 kg) Smoked and Pulled Pork (page 187), hot, chopped
8 servings Thai jasmine rice
¼ cup (40 g) fried shallots
¼ cup (20 g) chopped Thai basil

1. Preheat oven to 400°F (204°C). Line a baking sheet with parchment paper.
2. In a large mixing bowl, combine vegetable oil, soy sauce, turmeric powder, garlic powder, lime juice, sugar, white pepper, and chili flakes. Add in broccoli and bell peppers. Mix well, making sure everything is evenly coated.
3. Spread vegetables out on baking sheet so they are not touching. Roast for 15 to 18 minutes, flipping halfway through until vegetables are lightly caramelized and browned.
4. Add Thai Penang curry sauce to a large saucepan and warm through over medium heat while stirring. Add in roasted vegetables while stirring and bring to a low simmer. Curry is ready.
5. To serve, scoop a portion of jasmine rice into one side of a bowl. Pour a ladle of Penang curry and vegetables onto the empty side of the bowl. Add a healthy handful, about 4 to 5 ounces (113 to 142 g), of pulled pork on top of the Penang curry and vegetables, and then ladle extra curry broth over the pulled pork. Garnish with fried shallots and chopped Thai basil.

Serves 4

PAD KRAPOW PULLED PORK *with* FRIED EGG

Pad krapow is Thailand's great equalizer. This is a beloved dish that transcends social boundaries. Its ubiquitous presence, from upscale restaurants to humble street vendors, speaks to its universal appeal. The allure of pad krapow lies not only in its irresistible flavors but also in its accessibility and affordability. It's a culinary cornerstone, and it has become a huge part of Thai food culture. I remember having it for breakfast when I was traveling around Bangkok, and it made me wish this was a regular breakfast item I could find in the states—not to mention for lunch or dinner. In our recipe, the runny fried eggs, the herby, fragrant kick, and the crispy, juicy pulled pork, all crowning a bed of fluffy jasmine rice, truly creates a thing of beauty. —Sean

For the pad krapow sauce:

¼ cup (76 g) oyster sauce
2 tablespoons (30 ml) fish sauce
2 tablespoons (30 ml) soy sauce
1 tablespoon (15 ml) dark soy sauce
1 tablespoon (12 g) palm sugar or brown sugar
4 cloves garlic, minced
4 red Thai chilies, thinly sliced
½ cup (20 g) roughly chopped Thai basil (sub Thai holy basil if you can find it)

1 tablespoon (15 ml) vegetable oil
1½ pounds (680 g) Smoked and Pulled Pork, cold, shredded (page 187)
4 servings Thai jasmine rice
4 eggs, cooked sunny-side up until edges are crispy
4 lime wedges
4 Thai chilies, sliced thinly
¼ cup (10 g) Thai basil leaves

1. Make the pad krapow sauce: In a medium saucepan on low to medium heat, combine all sauce ingredients except Thai basil. Mix well on a low simmer for 3 to 4 minutes, until sauce begins to slightly thicken. Turn off heat and slowly stir in Thai basil to lightly wilt. Set aside.
2. In a large pan, heat vegetable oil on medium to high heat. Add shredded pulled pork and cook until the edges are crispy, 3 to 4 minutes. Add in pad krapow sauce evenly over pork in the pan and continue cooking and mixing for 3 to 4 minutes or until the sauce begins to caramelize on the pork.
3. Serve with a scoop of jasmine rice, a crispy runny fried egg, lime wedge, Thai chilies, and basil!

NOTE:
The pulled pork should be made the day before. This recipe calls for cold pulled pork.

Serves 4

HONEY SRIRACHA PULLED PORK SANDWICH *with* PICKLED GREEN PAPAYA *and* PENANG MAYO

On the surface, this seems like a simple, basic pulled pork sandwich—which wouldn't be a bad thing. But this banger of a sandwich adds a crunchy and tangy pickled green papaya as well as a spicy, sweet honey sriracha sauce to level up an already great sandwich. This sandwich is the unofficial sponsor for our Curry Boys back-of-house crew, as they seemingly have it for "staff meal" 75 percent of the time. Special shout-out to Chef Richard for this creation!

1 tablespoon (15 g) Thai Penang curry paste
1 tablespoon (14 g) mayonnaise (we like Duke's)
4 soft sandwich buns (we like a Martin's potato bun)
¼ cup (56 g) unsalted butter, softened
1½ pounds (680 g) Smoked and Pulled Pork, hot (page 187)
¼ cup (80 g) Honey Sriracha Sauce (page 46)
2 cups (472 g) Filipino Pickled Green Papaya and Carrot (page 106)

1. Combine Penang curry paste and mayonnaise in a small bowl and mix thoroughly. Set aside in the refrigerator.
2. Toast the sandwich buns in a pan over medium heat with butter until golden brown.
3. Assemble the sandwiches by brushing the top and bottom of each bun with the Penang curry mayo, then divide the pulled pork between the 4 sandwiches. Drizzle the pork with the honey sriracha sauce, and then top with a heaping portion of the pickled green papaya and carrot. Top with the top bun and enjoy!

Serves 4

NAM JIM JAEW PARTY RIBS

We call these "party ribs" because they are great for a party. Go figure. Individually sliced, crisped, and caramelized in a brown sugar and tamarind sauce, these ribs are so uniquely delicious that you may no longer need to make anything else for your next tailgate, backyard BBQ, or office potluck. And when your coworkers ask you about these complex flavors, you can tell them that you came up with this Thai-inspired sauce all by yourself because you're just a well-traveled, fun person. Then, you'll forever be known as the fun party person who brings fun party ribs!

1 rack St. Louis–style pork spareribs, about 3 pounds (1.4 kg)
¼ cup (25 g) Curry Boys BBQ Pork Rub (page 38)
¼ cup (56 g) unsalted butter, melted
⅓ cup (75 g) light brown sugar
3 tablespoons (60 g) honey
½ cup (118 ml) Nam Jim Jaew (page 168)
1 tablespoon (10 g) fried shallots
1 tablespoon (3 g) thinly sliced green onions
1 lime, quartered

1. Preheat your smoker to 275°F (135°C).
2. Pat the rack of ribs dry with paper towels. Trim off any excess skirt meat from the backside of the rack of ribs, and then slice each rib individually. Season the sliced ribs with the pork rub, ensuring that all 4 sides of each individual rib are evenly seasoned.
3. Place the individual ribs in your preheated smoker, meat-side up, and smoke at 275°F (135°C) for roughly 1½ hours, or until the ribs have a nice mahogany appearance and are reading 170°F (77°C) when a thermometer probe is inserted into the thickest part of the meat.
4. Remove the ribs from the smoker and place them in a foil pan. Add melted butter, brown sugar, honey, and nam jim jaew sauce to the ribs. Mix with your hands until everything is nicely coated. Cover the pan with aluminum foil and return to the smoker.
5. Continue smoking at 275°F (135°C) until the ribs are nice and tender and have developed good caramelization, which takes roughly 45 minutes. Remove the pan from the oven and, using tongs, arrange the ribs on a platter. Garnish with fried shallots, thinly sliced green onions, and lime wedges, and serve!

Serves 4

LEMONGRASS *and* OYSTER SAUCE PORK SPARERIBS

Juicy pork ribs basted with a sweet and savory sauce always make for a deliciously primal eating experience. I personally love eating these ribs with a side of tangy jeow som and white rice. In fact, I think most meat should be accompanied with a side of white rice. Pardon my extremely Asian take, but you're telling me that a side of white rice wouldn't be perfect at a Brazilian churrascaria or a steak house?! Rice is life, baby! —Sean

1 rack pork spareribs, about 4 pounds (1.8 kg)
¼ cup (25 g) Curry Boys BBQ Pork Rub (page 38)
2 cups (475 ml) Mama Ho's Vietnamese All-Purpose Meat Marinade (page 41)
2 tablespoons (2 g) chopped cilantro
1 tablespoon (10 g) fried shallots
Jeow Som (page 53), optional
4 portions Thai jasmine rice, optional

1. Preheat your smoker to 250°F (121°C).
2. Pat the ribs dry with paper towels. Trim ribs by removing the chine bone and squaring up the rack. Remove the excess skirt meat from the backside of the ribs. To season the ribs, apply a generous coating of pork rub to each side, ensuring the edges are well-seasoned.
3. Place the ribs in your smoker, meat-side up, as far away from the fire source as possible. If you are smoking on a relatively small smoker, consider placing a small water pan or even a dense piece of firewood between the ribs and the firebox to absorb some of the radiant heat and allow for a more even and consistent cook. Smoke ribs at 250°F (121°C) for 3 hours. At the 3-hour mark, use a silicone brush to brush your ribs with the marinade every 30 minutes until finished. Ribs will take approximately 6 hours to finish.
4. You can check your ribs for doneness using the "Bend Test" . . . Using gloves, pick up the rack in the center. When the ribs are finished, they will droop over the sides of your hand, and the meat should start to crack and pull away, without completely falling apart. For a general guideline, you are looking for the ribs to reach an internal temperature of 200°F to 203°F (93°C to 95°C) when a thermometer probe is slid into the thickest part of the meat. Wrap the ribs in foil, and allow them to rest for at least 15 minutes before slicing.
5. Slice the ribs by the bone, arrange the rack of sliced ribs on a platter, and garnish with cilantro and fried shallots. Best served drizzled with some jeow som (page 53) and accompanied by steamed jasmine rice.

PRO TIP:

You can also purchase your spareribs pretrimmed. These will be known as "St. Louis–style" pork spareribs, so look for them at your local grocery store if you prefer not to trim the ribs yourself.

Serves **4**

THE CURRY BOYS BBQ "PRIKRIB" SANDWICH

Prik means "chili" or "peppers" in Thailand, and if you know anything about us, we love ourselves a little bit of spice. We also love ourselves a couple of golden arches—two to be specific! The McDonald's McRib sandwich is a polarizing menu item among the BBQ community. Some love it. Some hate it. Some love it ironically. Some still just hate it. But there is something to be said about the sandwich's myth. It has stood the test of time and has become part of the fabric of the nostalgic tapestry of our lives. Our recipe pays homage to the original sandwich, but elevates it with high-quality protein, a perfect smoke, and the infusion of incredibly bright, spicy Thai flavors. It is both comforting and challenging; familiar, yet novel. I'm loving it.

1 rack St. Louis–style pork spareribs, about 3 pounds (1.4 kg)
¼ cup (25 g) Curry Boys BBQ Pork Rub (page 38)
2 cups + ¼ cup (500 + 64 g) Colby's Famous Thai-Texas Lemongrass BBQ Sauce (page 35)
4 seeded hamburger buns (we like Martin's "Big Marty")
¼ cup (56 g) unsalted butter, softened
1 cup (160 g) very thinly sliced white onion
½ cup (72 g) sliced jalapeños
1 cup (143 g) Curry Boys BBQ Tangy Pickled Cucumbers (page 108)
½ cup (120 g) sriracha, optional

1. Preheat your smoker to 250°F (121°C).
2. Pat the rack of ribs dry with paper towels. Ensure the ribs have been trimmed properly, with no brisket bone flap meat or rib tips remaining. Flip the ribs over to the backside, and using a boning knife, gently make shallow incisions down both sides of each bone. Doing this will allow the bones to be removed much more easily later in the recipe. Season the ribs on both sides with the pork rub.
3. Place the ribs in the smoker, bone-side down, and as far away from the fire source as possible. Smoke at 250°F (121°C) for 4 hours. Carefully remove the ribs from the smoker and lay them on 2 sheets of 18 x 24-inch (46 x 61 cm) heavy-duty foil. Tightly wrap the ribs in the foil and return to the smoker. Continue to smoke the wrapped ribs for 2 hours.
4. Remove the ribs from the smoker and unwrap. Allow the ribs to rest for 10 minutes, and then, carefully, you should be able to easily pull the bones away from the meat. Once the ribs have cooled enough to work with, cut the slab of boneless rib meat into 4 equal sections. Very carefully dunk each section of rib meat into the lemongrass BBQ sauce, coating it thoroughly, and then gently wrap each section in a small sheet of foil. Set aside.
5. Slice open the hamburger buns and brush the softened butter on each side. Toast the buns in a pan over medium heat until golden brown.
6. Remove the portions of rib meat from the foil packs and place 1 on each bun. Top each sandwich with the remaining lemongrass BBQ sauce and then layer with the sliced white onions, sliced jalapeños, and pickles. Drizzle with sriracha if desired for an extra kick of heat!

Serves 4 TO 6

BRAISED SMOKED PORK BELLY

Bangkok has a massive Chinatown—one of the biggest in the world. So, it is no surprise that the Chinese influence on the Thai culinary scene is also massive. This particular pork belly dish is incredibly popular in both China and Thailand, but we take it up a notch by smoking the pork belly first to infuse it with a gentle layer of mellowing smoke. The dish itself is quite rich, so the addition of smoke and the Thai chilies does a great job of tempering the dish a bit. I particularly love this dish with plain white rice and a side of pickles! —Sean

1 pound (454 g) boneless pork belly, skin-on if possible
1½ tablespoons (9 g) Curry Boys BBQ Pork Rub (page 38)
2 tablespoons (30 ml) vegetable oil
½ cup (96 g) packed palm sugar or brown sugar
3 to 4 thick slices of fresh ginger (⅛-inch [3 mm] thick)
2 whole scallions, roughly chopped
3 cloves garlic, smashed
⅓ cup (79 ml) rice wine (preferably Shaoxing wine)
¼ cup (60 ml) light soy sauce
¼ cup (60 ml) dark soy sauce
1 tablespoon (15 ml) fish sauce
3 cups (710 ml) water
1 star anise
⅓ cup (53 g) fried shallots
1 to 2 Thai chilies, optional

1. The pork belly can be made the day before! Preheat your smoker to 250°F (121°C).
2. Pat the pork belly dry with paper towels. Season both sides of the pork belly with the pork rub.
3. Place the pork belly in the smoker, fat-side up, as far away from the fire source as possible. Smoke for 3 to 4 hours, or until the meat reaches an internal temperature of 190°F (88°C) and is probe-tender. A meat thermometer should slide in and out with little to no resistance, like poking warm butter. Remove the pork belly from the smoker and allow it to rest for at least 30 minutes or overnight.
4. Slice the rested pork belly into 1-inch (2.5 cm) cubes and refrigerate until cold.
5. Heat oil in a large wok or saucepan over medium heat. Place the pork belly onto the pan—ensuring they are not stacked and that they are all making direct contact with the bottom of the pan. Cook the pork belly, without turning it, until 1 side is lightly browned, about 1 minute. Flip the pork belly pieces over onto the opposite side and cook until lightly browned, about 1 to 2 minutes. Remove the pork belly from the pan and set it aside.
6. In the same pan, add sugar and cook until it melts and looks syrupy. Be careful not to burn the sugar. If the sugar burns, clean your pan and start fresh. Add pork belly pieces, ginger, scallions, and garlic, making sure everything is coated, sizzling, and fragrant. Cook and stir occasionally for 3 to 5 minutes. Add rice wine, light soy sauce, dark soy sauce, fish sauce, and water. Stir to incorporate it all. Make sure the sugar is fully dissolved and incorporated.
7. Bring it to a boil and then add star anise, fried shallots, and Thai chilies, if you're looking for an extra kick of spice. Reduce the heat to a gentle simmer. Cover and cook until the pork is red colored, cooked through, and super tender, at least 1 to 2 hours. When the sauce has thickened and the pork belly is tender, it is ready to serve.

Serves 4

SMOKED PORK BELLY *BÁNH MÌ*

I'll fight anyone who doesn't think a bánh mì sandwich belongs in the Mount Rushmore of sandwiches. This classic Vietnamese sandwich has everything—crunch, tang, sweetness, umami, and spice—without feeling forced or "too much." Adding a fatty and smoky element helps the sandwich for our personal taste preferences, but if I'm being honest, the sandwich, in its original form, is perfect as it is. —Sean

2 pounds (907 g) boneless and skinless pork belly
2 tablespoons (13 g) Curry Boys BBQ Pork Rub (page 38)
2 cups (475 ml) Mama Ho's Vietnamese All-Purpose Meat Marinade (page 41)

For the pickled vegetables:

½ cup (118 ml) rice vinegar
¼ cup (60 ml) water
2 tablespoons (30 g) sugar
1 teaspoon salt
1 cup (116 g) peeled and julienned daikon
1 cup (110 g) peeled and julienned carrots
½ cup (60 g) peeled and julienned cucumber

½ cup (115 g) mayonnaise (we prefer Duke's)
1 tablespoon (15 g) sriracha
1 teaspoon lime juice
1 teaspoon fish sauce
4 crusty baguettes, split
¼ cup (56 g) unsalted butter
½ cup (8 g) fresh cilantro leaves
½ cup (72 g) sliced jalapeños
½ cup (20 g) fresh Thai basil leaves
½ cup (120 g) sriracha, optional

1. The pork belly can be made the day before! Preheat your smoker to 250°F (121°C). Pat the pork belly dry with paper towels. Season both sides of the pork belly liberally with the pork rub. Place the pork belly in the smoker, fat-side up, as far away from the fire source as possible. Smoke for 3 to 4 hours, or until the meat reaches an internal temperature of 190°F (88°C) and is probe-tender. A meat thermometer should slide in and out with little to no resistance, like poking warm butter. Remove the pork belly from the smoker and allow it to rest for at least 30 minutes or overnight.
2. Increase the temperature of your smoker or preheat it to 300°F (150°C). Slice the rested pork belly into ¼-inch (6 mm) slices. Dip the slices in the marinade, and arrange on a sheet tray in a single layer. Place the tray of sliced and marinated pork belly in the smoker. Smoke for 10 minutes, then flip, brush with the remaining marinade, and continue smoking for an additional 10 minutes. Remove the sliced pork belly from the smoker and rest until needed.
3. Make the pickled vegetables: In a bowl, combine vinegar, water, sugar, and salt. Whisk together until sugar dissolves. Add daikon, carrots, and cucumber to the vinegar mixture and let sit for at least 30 minutes.
4. Mix mayonnaise, sriracha, lime juice, and fish sauce in a small bowl. Cover and refrigerate. Slice and lightly toast the 4 baguettes with butter in a pan over medium heat until golden brown. Spread chili mayo on both sides of each baguette. Layer the sandwiches with the sliced smoked pork belly, pickled vegetables, fresh cilantro, jalapeños, and Thai basil. Drizzle with sriracha if desired. Enjoy best with a cold Bia Hanoi!

Serves 4

FILIPINO-STYLE SMOKED PORK BELLY LECHON

I still vividly remember having lechon on a balmy evening in Cebu, Philippines—the city alive with the sounds of motorbikes and Jeepneys rolling by the vendor—during a backpacking trip around the Philippines with Andrew Ho. The thing about traveling in Southeast Asia is that there is no shortage of incredible smells that usually lead to unbelievable meals. That's what happened to us on one fateful night. The smell of the pork belly caramelizing was too much for us to simply pass up. When we tried it, that crispy pork belly was just incredible—the perfect mix of salty, fatty, and crunchy that hits you right away. Honestly, it's easy to lose yourself with lechon; you just keep wanting more and more. —Sean

For the marinade:

3 tablespoons (45 ml) soy sauce
2 tablespoons (30 ml) fish sauce
1 tablespoon (10 g) minced garlic
1 tablespoon (15 g) brown sugar
1 tablespoon (6 g) five-spice powder
1 tablespoon (7 g) onion powder
2 teaspoons black pepper
2 tablespoons (30 ml) apple cider vinegar

2 pounds (907 g) skin-on pork belly
Vegetable oil for deep-frying

For the dipping sauce:

2 tablespoons (30 ml) soy sauce
1 tablespoon (15 ml) rice vinegar
1 teaspoon white sugar
2 Thai chilies (adjust for spiciness preference)
1 clove garlic, minced

¼ cup (4 g) chopped cilantro

1. Make the marinade: In a large mixing bowl, add marinade ingredients. Combine and mix well. Slice pork belly into 5 or 6 long 1½-inch (3.8 cm)-wide strips. Add the pork belly to the marinade and make sure the pork belly is coated evenly. Cover and marinade for 4 hours, or overnight for best flavor results.
2. Heat smoker to 225°F (107°C). Smoke pork belly fat-side up for 3 to 4 hours or until international temperature reaches 190°F (88°C). Set aside. Refrigerate smoked pork belly for 4 hours or until completely cooled. With a sharp knife, poke the top of the pork belly skin evenly in lines to score the meat.
3. In a large pot for frying, add 3 to 4 inches (7.6 to 10.2 cm) of vegetable oil and bring to 350°F (180°C). Add pork belly into oil skin-side down, frying for 8 to 12 minutes until pork belly is golden brown and develops a beautiful crisp. Flip pork belly over as needed for even frying. Be careful not to burn because the pork belly will already be browned from the smoking! Remove from oil and place on a large plate with paper towels to drain excess oil.
4. Make the dipping sauce: In a small mixing bowl, add dipping sauce ingredients. Combine and mix well until sugar is dissolved.
5. Slice hot pork belly into 1-inch (2.5 cm) cubes or chunks and plate neatly on a large serving platter. Garnish with chopped cilantro and serve with a dipping sauce on the side. This dish goes great with white jasmine rice and Vietnamese-Style "Đồ Chua" Pickled Carrot and Daikon (page 104) or Filipino Pickled Green Papaya and Carrot (page 106)!

Serves 4

PAD THAI with PAN-FRIED SMOKED PORK BELLY

When you think of Thai food, what dishes immediately come to mind? If you said, "Pad Thai," then you can thank the government of Thailand! In 2002, the Thai government launched its plan for culinary diplomacy—opening Thai restaurants and using food as a means of expanding its culture to all parts of the world. This is why you see so many Thai restaurants with similar menus across the United States. It's a beautiful thing to witness because in just over two decades, we have already seen the evolution of Thai food—beyond what was originally envisioned. More niche Thai dishes are being featured than ever before, and multicultural takes on the cuisine have also been popularized. This is where we come in. We've taken one of our favorite cuts of meat, prepared it in a way that is native to Texas, and combined it with a dish synonymous with Thailand. The result? An organic and fresh take on an already incredible dish.

1½ pounds (680 g) boneless and skinless pork belly
1½ tablespoons (9 g) Curry Boys BBQ Pork Rub (page 38)
1 tablespoon + ¼ cup (15 ml + 60 ml) vegetable oil, divided

For the sauce:

¼ cup (48 g) palm sugar or brown sugar
¼ cup (60 ml) fish sauce
¼ cup (65 g) tamarind paste
2 tablespoons (38 g) oyster sauce
1 tablespoon (15 ml) soy sauce
1 tablespoon (4 g) Thai chili flakes or powder (adjust to spiciness preference)

Ingredients continued

1. The pork belly can be made the day before! Preheat your smoker to 250°F (121°C).
2. Pat the pork belly dry with paper towels. Season both sides of the pork belly with the pork rub.
3. Place the pork belly in the smoker, fat-side up, as far away from the fire source as possible. Smoke for 3 to 4 hours, or until the meat reaches an internal temperature of 190°F (88°C) and is probe-tender. A meat thermometer should slide in and out with little to no resistance, like poking warm butter. Remove the pork belly from the smoker and allow it to rest for at least 30 minutes or overnight.
4. Slice the rested pork belly into 1-inch (2.5 cm) cubes and refrigerate until cold.
5. In a large pan, heat 1 tablespoon (15 ml) of vegetable oil on medium to high heat. Add smoked cold or room-temperature cubed pork belly and cook until the edges are crispy, 3 to 4 minutes. Remove from pan and set to the side.
6. Make the sauce: In a small mixing bowl, combine sauce ingredients. Set to the side.

Continued

Continued from previous page

6 cloves garlic, minced
4 eggs, beaten
4 servings cooked medium-wide rice noodles
2 cups (100 g) mung bean sprouts, divided
1 cup (48 g) chopped green onions
¼ cup (35 g) crushed peanuts
8 lime wedges
¼ cup (4 g) chopped cilantro
1 bunch green onion, dark green end pieces
Thai chili powder or flakes (adjust to spiciness preference)

7. In a large wok or pan, heat ¼ cup (60 ml) vegetable oil on medium to high heat. Add garlic and sauté for 30 seconds. Make sure not to burn! Slide garlic to one side of the wok. Pour in eggs and scramble on the empty side of the pan. Add cooked rice noodles and mix everything together well. Add sauce mixture evenly over noodles, making sure everything is coated, and cook evenly for 2 minutes. Mix in crispy pork belly, 1 cup (50 g) of mung bean sprouts, and chopped green onions, and continue mixing and cooking for another 2 to 3 minutes.
8. Garnish with crushed peanuts, lime wedges, chopped cilantro, green onion end pieces, the rest of the mung bean sprouts, and Thai chili flakes!

Serves 4

SWEET, STICKY, and SPICY PORK BELLY BURNT ENDS

A fan favorite special that we have on certain weekends at Curry Boys, this Pork Belly recipe will put you in vacation mode with a single, decadent bite! Out of all the ingredients, the lime and the fish sauce are the real winners and probably the reason why you can pop these burnt ends into your mouth like candy. Without them, pork belly can sometimes be too rich and fatty, but with just enough citrus and funk, the entire bite becomes balanced, nuanced, and beautifully complex.

4 pounds (1.8 kg) boneless and skinless pork belly (see note)
2 tablespoons (13 g) Curry Boys BBQ Pork Rub (page 38)

For the sauce:

¼ cup (85 g) honey
¼ cup (60 g) brown sugar
¼ cup (60 ml) fish sauce
¼ cup (76 g) oyster sauce
2 tablespoons (30 ml) dark soy sauce
2 tablespoons (30 ml) lime juice
2 tablespoons (30 g) sriracha
3 cloves garlic, minced
1 teaspoon grated ginger
2 teaspoons cornstarch
2 tablespoons (30 ml) water

Ingredients continued

1. Preheat your smoker to 250°F (121°C).
2. Pat the pork belly dry with paper towels. Season both sides of the pork belly with the pork rub.
3. Place the pork belly in the smoker fat-side up, as far away from the fire source as possible. Smoke for 3 to 4 hours, or until the meat reaches an internal temperature of 190°F (88°C) and is probe-tender. A meat thermometer should slide in and out with little to no resistance, like poking warm butter. Remove the pork belly from the smoker and allow it to rest for at least 30 minutes. Then refrigerate overnight.
4. The next day, preheat your smoker to 275°F (135°C).
5. Make the sauce: Combine all sauce ingredients except cornstarch and water in a small saucepan over medium-low heat. Whisk together until the brown sugar is dissolved and the mixture starts to bubble. Mix cornstarch and water in a small bowl to form a slurry, then slowly pour the slurry into the sauce while whisking constantly. Simmer while whisking for 2 minutes to slightly thicken the sauce. Pour the sauce into a small cup or bowl and set aside.

NOTE:
The pork belly should be started the day before.

Continued

Continued from previous page

¼ cup (12 g) thinly sliced green onion
¼ cup (7.5 g) crushed pork cracklings
2 limes, quartered

6. Remove the presmoked pork belly from the refrigerator and slice, then cube into 1 to 1½-inch (2.5 to 3.8 cm) cubes. Put the pork belly cubes in a pan and add the sauce. Toss to mix well, ensuring everything is coated nicely. Ensure the cubes are arranged in a single layer in the pan.
7. Place the pan in the smoker and smoke for 2½ hours, opening halfway to flip each individual cube over once. After 2½ hours, the pork belly burnt ends should be tender and nicely caramelized, with a crispy exterior. Remove the pan from the smoker and allow to rest for 10 to 15 minutes.
8. Using tongs, remove the pork belly burnt ends from the pan and arrange on a serving platter. Drizzle the sauce from the pan over the pork and garnish with thinly sliced green onions and crushed pork cracklings. Serve with lime wedges.

Serves 4

LAOTIAN-INSPIRED SMOKED PORK MEATBALL SANDWICH

I absolutely adore meatballs, and really any kind of food that comes in ball form (arancini, onigiri, and cake pops, to name a few). I also have an obsession with sandwiches. So, given this context, it should be no surprise that I love meatball subs or sandwiches. When you add in the fact that this is a Southeast Asian–inspired version, it is as if the Avengers have assembled inside of my mouth. It's a goddamn culinary cross-over that is so well-balanced, it feels like it was always meant to be. —Sean

For the meatballs:

1½ pounds (680 g) ground pork
6 cloves garlic, minced
3 tablespoons (30 g) finely minced shallots
1½ tablespoons (7 g) finely minced lemongrass
1½ tablespoons (29 g) oyster sauce
1½ tablespoons (22 ml) fish sauce
1½ teaspoons soy sauce
1½ teaspoons palm sugar or brown sugar
¾ teaspoon white pepper
1½ tablespoons (5 g) toasted rice powder (page 52)

½ cup (55 g) shredded carrot
½ cup (88 g) shredded green papaya
2 tablespoons + 4 teaspoons (30 ml + 20 ml) Jeow Som (page 53), divided
1 teaspoon white sugar
Pinch salt
4 medium sandwich baguettes (Bolillo rolls work!)
½ cup (20 g) chopped Thai basil
½ cup (8 g) chopped cilantro
1 cucumber, sliced
2 red Thai chilies, sliced thinly

For the chili mayo:

¼ cup (56 g) mayonnaise
1 teaspoon Thai chili paste

1. Preheat smoker to 225°F (107°C).
2. Make the meatballs: In a large mixing bowl, combine all meatball ingredients. Mix well to make sure everything is coated evenly. Using clean hands or wearing gloves, roll pork mixture into 1-inch (2.5 cm) balls. Place on a plate. Place meatballs on smoker grates, making sure they are not touching. Smoke for 50 to 60 minutes or until internal temperature reaches 160°F (71°C).
3. In a large mixing bowl, combine shredded carrot and papaya, 2 tablespoons (30 ml) of jeow som sauce, sugar, and salt. Mix together well and set to the side.
4. Make the chili mayo: Mix together the ingredients for the chili mayo and set aside.
5. Toast baguettes and slice longways. Spread chili mayo on both halves of baguette. Carefully stuff baguettes with smoked meatballs, Thai basil, cilantro, cucumbers, carrot and papaya slaw, and Thai red chilies. Drizzle 1 teaspoon of jeow som sauce over each sandwich and enjoy!

Serves 8

CURRY QUESO HOT DOG *with* SMOKED HOT LINK

OKAY, THIS IS MY ABSOLUTE FAVORITE THING ON THE MENU AT CURRY BOYS BBQ, AND I'M GOING TO TYPE IN ALL CAPS TO LET YOU KNOW HOW SERIOUS I AM. THE JUICY SNAP OF THE SAUSAGE, THE VELVETY CURRY QUESO, AND THE CRISPY WHITE ONION—ALL ADORNING A SOFT, CLOUDLIKE POTATO ROLL—IS ABSOLUTELY ONE OF THE GREATEST BITES OF FOOD IN THE WORLD. I KNOW WE HAVE BADASS BRISKET AND SUCCULENT PULLED PORK AT THE RESTAURANT, BUT THIS HOT DOG GIVES ME LIFE. THANK YOU FOR LISTENING TO MY TED TALK. —Sean

8 spicy pork sausage links
8 hot dog buns (we prefer Martin's potato rolls)
2 cups (475 ml) Curry Queso (page 56)
½ cup (80 g) finely sliced white onion
½ cup (8 g) chopped cilantro
¼ cup (40 g) fried shallots

1. Preheat smoker to 225°F (107°C).
2. Place sausage links onto smoker grates, making sure they are not touching. For precooked sausage, smoke for 1½ to 2 hours. For raw sausage, smoke for 2½ to 3 hours. Remove from smoker when sausages have a nice plump look to them and they have an internal temperature of 160°F (71°C).
3. On a large serving platter, open and lay out 8 hot dog bugs in a row. Insert smoked sausage link into each bun. Ladle 2 ounces (60 ml) of queso over each sausage link. Garnish liberally with white onion, cilantro, and fried shallots.

Serves 4

SMOKED LAMB SHANK *and* THAI MASSAMAN CURRY *with* ROASTED CARROTS *and* POTATOES

What's the sexiest thing you can think of? The correct answer is "smoked lamb shank and massaman curry," but we'd also accept "Andrew Ho," "Andrew Samia," or "Sean Wen" as correct answers too. Because massaman curry is inherently a mixture of South Asian and Southeast Asian flavors, and because the smoked lamb is an added element of Texas barbecue, each spoonful of this dish covers thousands of miles of delicious cultural diversity. It's one of our most popular weekly specials at Curry Boys BBQ because it's a luxurious dish served in a humble way: fragrant rice, fork-tender lamb shank, and a rich curry. What's not to love?

4 lamb shanks, about 1 pound (454 g) each

For the rub:

1 tablespoon (18 g) kosher salt
1 tablespoon (6 g) 16-mesh black pepper
1 teaspoon garlic powder
½ teaspoon ground coriander
¼ teaspoon white pepper

¼ cup (60 ml) water
¼ cup (60 ml) apple cider vinegar
½ cup (118 ml) beef broth

Ingredients continued

1. Carefully trim off any extra fat or silver skin from the lamb shanks. Leave a small piece of the fat cap on each lamb shank so the fat renders during smoking.
2. Make the rub: In a small mixing bowl, combine ingredients for the rub. Mix well.
3. Season each lamb shank liberally with the rub and make sure everything is coated evenly. Place lamb shanks evenly spaced out on a wire rack on a sheet pan and refrigerate uncovered for 8-plus hours or overnight.
4. Preheat smoker to 250°F (121°C). Combine water and apple cider vinegar in a spray bottle.
5. Take lamb shanks out of the refrigerator and place onto smoker grates bone-side down. Smoke for 3½ to 4 hours and then lightly spritz with water and apple cider vinegar mixture every hour. When the lamb shanks' internal temperature reaches 165°F to 170°F (71°C to 77°C) (a bark or crust should develop around this time), baste each shank lightly with beef broth and then wrap tightly in aluminum foil. Place lamb shanks back in smoker and continue smoking until internal temperature reaches 205°F (96°C) at the thickest part of the shank. This should take about 2 to 3 hours. Remove lamb shanks from smoker and allow to rest in an insulated cooler with the lid propped open a little or a warm oven (175°F [79°C]) for 30 to 45 minutes.
6. While the lamb shanks rest, preheat oven to 400°F (204°C). Line a baking sheet with parchment paper.

Continued

Continued from previous page

1 tablespoon (15 ml) vegetable oil
½ teaspoon salt
½ teaspoon turmeric powder
¼ teaspoon white pepper
1 cup (110 g) peeled and sliced carrots
2 medium or large potatoes, sliced into chunks
1⅛ quarts (1.1 L) Massaman Curry Sauce (page 31)
4 servings Thai jasmine rice
2 tablespoons (20 g) fried shallots
¼ cup (4 g) chopped cilantro
¼ cup (35 g) crushed roasted peanuts
¼ cup (20 g) Thai basil leaves
½ tablespoon chopped red Thai chilies (adjust to spiciness preference)
Crispy Garlic Chili Oil (page 45), optional
Curry Boys BBQ Tangy Pickled Cucumbers (page 108), optional

7. In a large mixing bowl, combine and mix vegetable oil, salt, turmeric powder, and white pepper. Add in carrots and potatoes and mix well, making sure vegetables are evenly coated. Spread vegetables out on a baking sheet so they are not touching. Roast in oven for 25 to 30 minutes, flipping halfway through until they are golden brown.
8. Heat massaman curry in a large saucepan over medium heat. Add in roasted carrots and potatoes while stirring and bring curry to a low simmer. Curry is ready.
9. To serve, scoop a portion of jasmine rice into one side of a large bowl. Pour a ladle of massaman curry and carrots and potatoes onto the empty side of the bowl. Add 1 smoked lamb shank into the massaman curry and roasted vegetables, and then ladle extra curry broth over the lamb shank. Garnish with fried shallots, a tiny bit of cilantro for color, crushed roasted peanuts, Thai basil, and red Thai chilies. Serve with chili oil and house pickles if you're wanting an extra flavor bomb!

Serves 4

THAI GREEN CURRY-MARINATED SMOKED RACK OF LAMB *with* MINT DIPPING SAUCE

Although lamb is an underutilized meat in Texas barbecue, it holds a special place in Andrew Samia's memories. He fondly recalls secretly sharing lamb chops under the dinner table with his Lebanese grandmother during Easter, both starving and impatient. When lamb is done well, it can stand toe to toe with any smoked protein. The slightly gamier notes of lamb can be muted by acidic and aromatic notes, making it the perfect protein for our marinade of green curry, soy, and lime juice. Once it is marinated and smoked, you'll love this juicy rack of lamb so much that you might even start sneaking a couple chops under the table before dinner starts!

1 rack of lamb with 8 bones, preferably frenched

For the marinade:

3 tablespoons (45 g) Thai green curry paste
1 tablespoon (15 ml) fish sauce
1 tablespoon (15 ml) dark soy sauce
1 tablespoon (15 ml) lime juice
1 tablespoon (15 g) coconut milk
1 tablespoon (12 g) palm sugar or brown sugar
1 tablespoon (1 g) chopped fresh cilantro
1 teaspoon ground cumin
1 teaspoon ground coriander
1 teaspoon turmeric powder
1 tablespoon (8 g) grated fresh ginger
2 cloves garlic, minced
1 tablespoon (5 g) lemongrass, finely chopped
1 Thai chili, finely minced

Ingredients continued

1. Pat the rack of lamb dry with paper towels.
2. Make the marinade: Combine all the marinade ingredients in a large mixing bowl and whisk until thoroughly incorporated.
3. Add the rack of lamb to the marinade and mix well to ensure even coverage. Cover and refrigerate for at least 4 hours, but preferably overnight for maximum flavor.

Continued

Continued from previous page

For the mint dipping sauce:

1 cup (96 g) fresh mint leaves
1 cup (16 g) fresh cilantro leaves
1 Thai green chili pepper, stem removed
3 slices ginger
3 cloves garlic
2 tablespoons (24 g) palm sugar or brown sugar
¼ cup (59 ml) rice vinegar
2 tablespoons (30 ml) water
½ teaspoon salt
3 tablespoons (45 ml) canola oil

4. Make the mint dipping sauce: Combine all the ingredients, except the canola oil, in a blender and blend until smooth. Slowly drizzle canola oil into the blender while continuing to blend to emulsify the sauce.
5. Preheat smoker to 225°F (107°C). Remove the lamb and marinade from the refrigerator. Scrape off any excess marinade from the meat and let it rest for 30 minutes before smoking.
6. Place the rack of lamb in the smoker bone-side down, as far away from the fire source as possible. Smoke at 225°F (107°C) for 1½ to 2 hours, or until the internal temperature reaches 125°F (52°C).
7. While the rack of lamb is smoking, prepare your grill for high heat by building a high bed of burned-down wood or lump charcoal.
8. When the lamb reaches an internal temperature of 125°F (52°C), remove it from the smoker to rest for 10 minutes before grilling. Grill your rack of lamb over high heat, flipping every minute, for approximately 4 minutes in total, to develop a good crust and bring the internal temperature up to 130°F (54°C) for medium-rare. Cook longer if desired. Let the rack of lamb rest for 15 minutes. Slice the rack into individual chops and serve with a side of mint dipping sauce.

chapter
9

SWEETS *and* DESSERTS

Makes 1 PAN, 9 X 9 X 2-INCH (23 X 23 X 5 CM), ABOUT 6 TO 10 SNACKS

THAI-INSPIRED MANGO *and* COCONUT RICE CRISPY SNACKS

Nothing is more nostalgic than a gooey rice crispy treat. As a kid, they were one of my favorite desserts. And as an adult? Still one of my favorite desserts. I'm just a sucker for anything sweet and fruity, and this recipe is exactly what I crave—a lovechild of mango sticky rice and a traditional puffed rice cereal treat. Taking a bite of this Thai-inspired treat will put you smack dab in the tropical paradise of Koh Samui while also reminding you to find joy in what you used to love as a child! —Sean

For the rice crispies:

¼ cup (56 g) unsalted butter, plus more as needed
10 ounces (283 g) marshmallows
1 teaspoon vanilla extract
½ teaspoon salt
½ cup (65 g) finely chopped dried mango
6 cups (162 g) puffed rice cereal

For the coconut drizzle:

½ cup (142 g) coconut cream
¼ cup (76 g) sweetened condensed milk
¼ teaspoon salt
½ teaspoon vanilla extract

½ cup (40 g) toasted sweet coconut flakes
¼ cup (41 g) diced fresh mango
1 teaspoon sesame seeds

1. Lightly grease or butter a 9 x 9 x 2-inch (23 x 23 x 5 cm) baking dish.
2. Make the rice crispies: In a large pot or saucepan, over low heat, melt butter. Add in marshmallows and stir until they are fully melted and a smooth consistency. Remove pan from heat and mix in vanilla extract, salt, and dried mango. Carefully fold in rice cereal, making sure everything is coated evenly. Pour mixture into the baking dish. Using a spatula, press mixture down to ensure mixture is evenly distributed in pan. You want the top to be flat. Let sit at room temperature for 45 minutes.
3. Make the coconut drizzle: In a small saucepan over low heat, whisk together coconut drizzle ingredients until smooth. Remove from heat and let cool for 5 to 10 minutes.
4. Once the rice crispies have set, cut into squares. Plate on small serving platters and drizzle coconut drizzle over the top. Garnish with toasted coconut flakes, diced fresh mango, and sesame seeds. We love it with the Smoked Brisket and Thai Green Curry (page 167) and Nam Jim Jaew Party Ribs (page 196)!

PRO TIP:

Be sure to use coconut cream, not coconut milk, in this recipe!

Serves 8

CALAMANSI PIE BARS *with* SMOKED GRAHAM CRACKER CRUST

Key lime pie is an extremely underrated pie. I can already hear everyone uttering under their breaths that it's a popular pie and definitely not underrated. But not everyone lives near the Florida Keys or is Florida-adjacent, okay?

This Calamansi pie bar is our version of a Key lime pie and a perfect dessert after a rich, hearty Texas barbecue feast. We substituted calamansi for Key limes, which are a small citrus native to Southeast Asia and particularly popular in the Philippines. Calamansi is a bit sweeter and less tart than Key limes.

1½ cups (180 g) graham cracker crumbs
⅓ cup (67 g) granulated sugar
6 tablespoons (86 g) salted butter, melted
4 ounces (113 g) cream cheese, room temperature
2 (14-ounce [397 g]) cans sweetened condensed milk
¾ cup (177 ml) fresh-squeezed calamansi juice
Zest of 2 calamansi, plus more as needed
2 cups (480 g) heavy whipping cream
¼ cup (30 g) powdered sugar
1 teaspoon pure vanilla extract

1. Preheat smoker and oven to 350°F (180°C).
2. Combine graham cracker crumbs, sugar, and melted butter in a medium bowl and press into an 8-inch (20 cm) square springform pan. Smoke the crust in your offset smoker for 10 minutes. Allow to cool before adding filling.
3. Add cream cheese to a mixing bowl and beat well with electric beaters until smooth. Add both cans of sweetened condensed milk, calamansi juice, and calamansi zest. Mix again until smooth. Pour the filling over the smoked and cooled graham cracker crust.
4. Bake in the oven for 10 minutes. Remove pan from oven and allow it to cool for 30 minutes. Then, refrigerate for at least 3 hours before serving, or overnight for best results!
5. Clean your mixing bowl and beaters and place them in the freezer for about 15 minutes to make things easier.
6. Pour heavy cream into the cold mixing bowl and beat on medium speed for about 2 minutes until it starts to thicken. Add powdered sugar and vanilla extract, then increase the speed to high and continue beating for about 2 to 4 minutes, or until stiff peaks form. Store in the refrigerator until ready to serve.
7. Slice pie into bars and serve with a dollop of fresh whipped cream and a fresh zest of calamansi.

Makes 1 PAN, 9 X 9 X 2-INCH (23 X 23 X 5 CM)

CHOCOLATE CHUNK *and* SMOKED PECAN BROWNIES À LA MODE *with* COCONUT CARAMEL

I'm going to try to refrain from saying "ooey-gooey" to describe this recipe, but Lord knows it'll be next to impossible. I'm not sure I've ever encountered a brownie I didn't like. It doesn't matter if it's Cosmic Brownies, some Betty Crocker brownie mix, a box of Trader Joe's Brownie Bites, your grandmother's secret brownie recipe, or your other grandmother's secret brownie recipe: If I see it, I'm going to gobble it up. You want to know something crazy? I don't even crave chocolate, but when I see a brownie or anything brownie adjacent, I'm only thinking about taking a bite into that decadent, fudgy, chewy dessert. This recipe in particular is as decadent, and as delicious, as it gets. However, there is still an emphasis on balance, as the brownie is layered with bits of crunchiness, a hint of smokiness, toasted nuttiness, and velvety, fudgy sweetness. When it's finished baking, what you get is a symphony of aromas and a bite that can be described by only a singular phrase: ooey-gooey. Oops. Couldn't resist it—much like this brownie. —Sean

For the coconut caramel:

1 cup (200 g) white sugar
¼ cup (60 ml) water
2 cups (448 g) coconut milk
¼ teaspoon kosher salt
1 teaspoon vanilla extract

1 cup (100 g) pecan halves

Ingredients continued

1. Make the coconut caramel: Add sugar and water to a saucepan. Mix once just to combine and then heat over medium heat without stirring. Cook until the sugar melts and turns a deep amber color. Remove pan from the heat and carefully add coconut milk. Whisk constantly until smooth. Return pan to low heat and simmer for 10 minutes, whisking constantly, until caramel thickens. Stir in kosher salt and vanilla extract and allow caramel to cool before transferring to a container and refrigerating until needed.
2. Preheat smoker to 250°F (121°C). Line a sheet tray with parchment paper, if desired.
3. Spread pecan halves on a sheet tray and smoke for 30 minutes. Remove from the smoker, allow to cool, then chop into pieces and set aside.
4. Preheat oven to 350°F (180°C). Rub butter on the bottom and sides of a 9 x 9 x 2-inch (23 x 23 x 5 cm) pan.

Continued

Continued from previous page

12 tablespoons (168 g) unsalted butter, plus more as needed
9 ounces (255 g) bittersweet chocolate chips
1½ cups (300 g) white sugar
1¼ cups (210 g) light brown sugar, lightly packed
3 eggs
2 egg yolks
¾ teaspoon kosher salt
1 teaspoon vanilla extract
1 cup (125 g) all-purpose flour
6 ounces (170 g) semisweet chocolate, cut into chunks

2 scoops vanilla bean ice cream per serving

5. Heat 2 inches (5 cm) or so of water in a small saucepan until simmering, then place a glass or stainless steel bowl over the pan. You want enough water to create steam for several minutes, but the water should not touch the bottom of the bowl. Add butter and bittersweet chocolate chips to the bowl and melt, stirring constantly until melted and smooth.
6. In a large mixing bowl, whisk together white sugar, light brown sugar, eggs, egg yolks, salt, and vanilla until smooth. Add melted butter and chocolate mixture to the mixing bowl and stir just to combine. Add flour evenly to the mixing bowl, and stir to combine. Fold in semisweet chocolate chunks and smoked and chopped pecans. Using a rubber spatula, scoop all of the brownie batter into the greased pan.
7. Bake in the oven for 40 to 45 minutes, or until a toothpick inserted into the center comes out as clean as you want it! Less clean equals gooier brownies. Remove the brownies from the oven and allow the pan to rest on a rack to cool for 45 minutes before serving. Top each brownie with 2 scoops of vanilla bean ice cream, drizzle with the coconut caramel, and enjoy!

THAI SWEET HAWAIIAN GLAZED BUNS *with* THAI TEA *and* MATCHA CUSTARD DIPS

Inspired by our dear friend, Chef Sam from Yaowarat, the Chinese-Thai restaurant in Portland, Oregon, these buns are not here to play! This recipe is a cheat code because sweet Hawaiian buns are already good on their own, but when paired with a little butter, a little condensed milk, and a little custard dip, your sweet tooth will evolve into a full-on sweet mouth. The smell alone is enough to make a person drop to their knees, but that first bite into the decadent, pillowy bun will turn any righteous man into a sinner. Sometimes it's fun to be bad.

12 sweet Hawaiian bread buns (should be 1 pack)
3 tablespoons (14 g) unsalted butter, melted
1 tablespoon (20 g) honey
1 tablespoon (19 g) sweetened condensed milk

For the Thai tea dip:

1 cup (235 ml) whole milk
½ cup (120 g) heavy cream
2 tablespoons (4 g) Thai tea mix or leaves (we prefer ChaTraMue)
2 egg yolks
2 tablespoons (26 g) white sugar
2 tablespoons (38 g) sweetened condensed milk
1 tablespoon (8 g) cornstarch
Pinch salt

Ingredients continued

1. Preheat oven to 375°F (191°C).
2. Slice buns as you would for sliders. Brush cut sides with melted butter. Toast buns with buttered-side up on a baking sheet until crispy and lightly golden.
3. In a small bowl, combine honey and sweetened condensed milk. Brush top of buns with honey mixture.
4. Make the Thai tea dip: In a small saucepan on low heat, mix milk, heavy cream, and Thai tea mix. Let simmer, stirring occasionally, for 6 to 8 minutes. Remove from heat and pour liquid through a fine strainer into a measuring cup or medium mixing bowl. In a separate medium mixing bowl, mix together egg yolks, sugar, sweetened condensed milk, and cornstarch. Slowly whisk Thai tea mixture into the egg mix until combined well. Pour mixture back into same small saucepan over medium heat and continue stirring until the mixture thickens. Remove from heat and stir in a pinch of salt for a nice balance. Cover and refrigerate before serving.

Continued

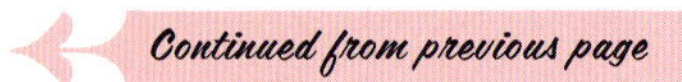
Continued from previous page

For the matcha custard dip:

1 cup (235 ml) whole milk
½ cup (120 g) heavy cream
2 tablespoons (38 g) sweetened condensed milk
2 egg yolks
2 tablespoons (26 g) white sugar
1 tablespoon (8 g) cornstarch
1½ teaspoons matcha powder
Pinch salt

5. Make the matcha custard dip: In a small saucepan on low heat, combine whole milk, heavy cream, and sweetened condensed milk, and stir to combine well until mixture is warm. Don't simmer or boil! In a separate medium mixing bowl, mix together egg yolks, sugar, cornstarch, and matcha powder. Whisk until smooth and combined well. Slowly whisk warm milk mixture into the egg mix until combined well. Pour mixture back into the same small saucepan over medium heat and continue stirring until the mixture thickens. Remove from heat and stir in a pinch of salt for a nice balance. Cover and refrigerate before serving.
6. Slice buns into sections of 2 and serve on a small/medium serving platter with a small sauce plate of each dipping custard. Goes great with our Pad See Ew with Smoked Beef Cheek Barbacoa (page 175)!

Serves 6

SMOKED VIETNAMESE COFFEE BREAD PUDDING

Andrew Samia goes nuts for coffee-flavored anything, and this dessert is no exception. He first introduced this dessert to us a couple years ago, and although I'm not a big coffee drinker, I could not get enough of the bread pudding! Smoking the bread pudding and adding a bit of bitterness from the coffee really mellows the intense sweetness of condensed milk and also ensures that this dessert does not feel too heavy or too rich. It is also genuinely easy to make and is a great introduction to the world of baking desserts. —Sean

6 cups (210 g) day-old brioche, cut into 1-inch (2.5 cm) cubes
2 (8.12-ounce [240 ml]) cans Vietnamese iced coffee (we like Mr. Brown Iced Coffee)
1 cup (240 g) half-and-half
1 cup (235 ml) sweetened condensed milk, divided
4 large eggs
2 teaspoons vanilla extract
¼ teaspoon kosher salt
3 tablespoons (42 g) unsalted butter, melted

1. Preheat oven to 300°F (150°C). Grease an 8 x 8 x 2-inch (20 x 20 x 5 cm) baking dish with cooking spray.
2. Lightly toast bread cubes in the oven on a sheet tray for 10 minutes to dry them out. Layer the dried bread cubes into the greased dish.
3. In a large bowl, combine iced coffee, half-and-half, ¾ cup (177 ml) of sweetened condensed milk, eggs, vanilla extract, kosher salt, and melted butter. Whisk together to create a custard.
4. Pour custard mixture evenly over bread cubes in the baking dish. Allow it to sit and absorb for at least 20 minutes while you preheat your smoker to 275°F (135°C).
5. Place the baking dish in the smoker, as far away from the fire source as possible, and smoke for 55 to 70 minutes, rotating 180 degrees halfway, until custard has set but is still slightly jiggly in the center. Remove the baking dish from the smoker and allow it to cool for 15 minutes before serving.
6. Drizzle with the remaining ¼ cup (60 ml) sweetened condensed milk and serve!

PRO TIPS:

Make the bread pudding the night before and allow it to soak overnight in the refrigerator before smoking the next day for best results. You can substitute Irish cream or coffee liqueur for the drizzled sweetened condensed milk for a boozy treat!

Makes 1 COBBLER, 8 X 8 X 2-INCH (20 X 20 X 5 CM)

SMOKED ASIAN PEAR COBBLER *with* WHITE CHOCOLATE *and* WALNUT COOKIE CRUST

Cobbler is already a superior dessert (dare I say, even better than pie?) because of its sweet and jammy fruit filling and crumbly, buttery crust. It truly is the epitome of comfort food. But why stop there? One fateful day while he was trimming and smoking meat, Andrew Samia had the idea of replacing traditional cobbler crust with his mother-in-law's famous cookie dough batter, and then also smoking the cobbler to add depth and cut through the sweetness. For the record, I've had these particular white chocolate and walnut cookies on their own, and they are honestly mind-blowing, so I cannot wait for you all to try this cobbler recipe! —Sean

For the fruit filling:

4 Asian pears, peeled, cored, and sliced
½ cup (115 g) light brown sugar
1 tablespoon (15 ml) fresh lime juice
1 teaspoon vanilla extract
½ teaspoon ground ginger
Pinch kosher salt
1 tablespoon (8 g) cornstarch

For the cookie dough batter:

1 (15-ounce [425 g]) package white cake mix
¼ cup (60 g) light brown sugar
1 large egg
1 cup (175 g) white chocolate chips
½ cup (60 g) chopped walnuts
¾ cup (177 ml) vegetable oil

2 scoops vanilla bean ice cream per serving, optional

1. Preheat your smoker to 325°F (163°C). Grease an 8 x 8 x 2-inch (20 x 20 x 5 cm) baking dish.
2. Make the fruit filling: Combine sliced Asian pears, brown sugar, lime juice, vanilla extract, ground ginger, kosher salt, and cornstarch in a large mixing bowl and mix well. Pour the Asian pear mixture into the greased baking dish and allow this to rest while you prepare the cobbler topping so that some of the juices start to release.
3. Make the cookie dough batter: Add all cookie dough batter ingredients to a mixing bowl and mix until well combined.
4. Drop spoonfuls of cookie dough batter evenly over the top of the Asian pears in the baking dish. Place the cobbler in the smoker, as far away from the fire as possible, and smoke at 325°F (163°C) for 30 minutes, rotating 180 degrees halfway through. Check at the 30-minute mark; you want to have a golden brown topping with a bubbly filling. If needed, rotate 180 degrees again and continue to smoke for an additional 15 to 30 minutes. Remove the cobbler from the smoker and allow it to rest for at least 10 minutes before serving.
5. To serve, scoop the cobbler, getting a good mixture of crust and filling, into a bowl, and top with a couple scoops of vanilla bean ice cream if desired!

Makes 1 CHEESECAKE, 9-INCH (23 CM) DIAMETER, TO SERVE 10 TO 12

SMOKED COCONUT CHEESECAKE

I have a confession. I've never been to the Cheesecake Factory, and I'm low-key embarrassed by that fact. I had a good buddy tell me his favorite thing there was a coconut cheesecake, so, to double-down on my embarrassment, that was the inspiration for this recipe. I figured if we were going to do a cheesecake, why not smoke it for that gentle smoke-kissed flavor too. And, good Lord, is this thing addictive. Again, I don't have a great benchmark in terms of how it compares with the Cheesecake Factory's version, but quite frankly, I don't care. —Sean

For the crust:

1½ cups (180 g) graham cracker crumbs
½ cup (40 g) unsweetened shredded coconut
¼ cup (50 g) white sugar
Pinch kosher salt
6 tablespoons (86 g) unsalted butter, melted
1 tablespoon (15 ml) melted coconut oil

For the filling:

24 ounces (680 g) cream cheese, room temperature
¾ cup (150 g) white sugar
1 cup (283 g) coconut cream
4 large eggs
2 teaspoons vanilla extract
1 cup (80 g) sweetened shredded coconut

½ cup (40 g) toasted coconut flakes

1. Preheat smoker to 300°F (150°C). Place the springform pan in a large roasting pan and fill the roasting pan with hot water until it comes halfway up the sides of the springform pan. Remove the springform pan.
2. Make the crust: Add the dry crust ingredients to a mixing bowl and stir until well combined. Add melted butter and continue stirring until the mixture is fully incorporated. Press the mixture evenly into a 9-inch (23 cm) springform pan. Brush the crust evenly with a thin layer of coconut oil before smoking. Set the pan in the smoker and smoke for 10 minutes to infuse the crust with smoke. Remove the pan from the smoker and set aside.
3. Make the filling: In a stand mixer, beat cream cheese and sugar until smooth and creamy. Next, add coconut cream, eggs, and vanilla extract, one at a time, mixing to incorporate fully after each addition. Evenly fold sweetened shredded coconut into filling mixture. Pour cheesecake filling mixture into the presmoked crust in the springform pan.
4. Carefully place the springform pan into the roasting pan and put the water bath in the smoker, as far away from the fire source as possible. Smoke the cheesecake at 300°F (150°C) for 1 hour and 20 minutes, and then check for doneness. The cheesecake is finished when the filling still has a slight wobble in the center, but should not be jiggling too much. You might need an additional 20 minutes. Remove the cheesecake from the smoker and allow it to cool to room temperature before refrigerating overnight. Garnish the cheesecake with toasted coconut flakes and serve!

Serves 6

THAI TEA MILKSHAKE *with* GRAHAM CRACKER *and* SMOKED COCONUT CRUMBLE

Is a milkshake a dessert or a beverage? This is like one of those "Is a hot dog a sandwich?" kind of things, and I'm strongly in the "milkshake is a dessert" camp. Why wouldn't it be? It's decadent, sweet, and something you crave at the end of the meal (or literally, any time of day). Now, I'm sure we have all had a vanilla, chocolate, or Oreo milkshake before. They're delicious. But if you are looking for an all-time, upper-echelon version of a milkshake, then you need to try this Thai tea milkshake with a crunchy graham cracker crumble. The Thai tea is inherently sweet due to the condensed milk, and the smoked coconut and graham cracker crumble adds another dimension of texture, aroma, and flavor! —Sean

For the smoked crumble:

2 tablespoons (10 g) shredded unsweetened coconut
3 tablespoons (23 g) graham cracker crumbs
1 tablespoon (12 g) palm sugar or brown sugar
Pinch salt
1 tablespoon (14 g) unsalted butter, melted

2 cups (473 ml) water
1 cup (32 g) Thai tea leaves or mix (we prefer ChaTraMue)
½ cup (100 g) sugar
2 cups (280 g) vanilla ice cream
½ cup (120 ml) evaporated milk or half-and-half
1 teaspoon vanilla extract
Pinch salt
½ cup (30 g) whipped cream (canned works fine!)

1. Prepare your smoker to cold-smoke at 85°F to 90°F (29°C to 32°C). Line a baking sheet with foil and a second baking sheet with parchment paper. Preheat oven to 325°F (163°C).
2. Make the smoked crumble: Cold-smoke shredded coconut on the baking sheet for 25 to 30 minutes. You are looking for a light cold smoke, not a full-on roasting. Remove from smoker and set to the side. In a medium mixing bowl, combine the rest of the dry smoked crumble ingredients. Slowly mix in melted butter, making sure everything is evenly coated. Spread crumble mixture onto the parchment paper–lined baking sheet and bake in the oven for 7 to 8 minutes. Flip or stir halfway through until mixture is crispy and golden. Set aside to cool before serving.
3. In a small pot, bring 2 cups (473 ml) of water to a boil. Add Thai tea leaves or mix and simmer on low for 4 to 5 minutes. Add in sugar and stir slowly until sugar is dissolved. Remove from heat and let steep for 10 minutes. Remove from heat and pour liquid through a fine strainer into a measuring cup or medium mixing bowl.
4. To a blender, add Thai tea mixture, ice cream, evaporated milk or half-and-half, vanilla extract, and salt. Blend until smooth and to your liking. Use your judgment on how you prefer your milkshakes!
5. Pour milkshake into 4 tall glasses and top with whipped cream and smoked coconut graham cracker crumble!

FLAN SOLO with GINGER COCONUT CARAMEL SAUCE

While Mexican flan is widely known, Vietnam also boasts a very popular flan dessert. Introduced during the French colonial era, flan has become deeply embedded in Vietnamese culinary tradition. Vietnamese flan has since evolved to include local ingredients, such as condensed milk and Vietnamese coffee, and can be found street side for only $0.33 USD! This recipe in particular is from Andrew Ho's mother-in-law, Betty, and is the perfect sweet treat at the end of a heavy BBQ feast. Rather than pouring Vietnamese coffee over the top of the flan—as they do in the streets of Ho Chi Minh—we opted for a decadent, yet still light, ginger coconut caramel sauce. Absolutely divine.

For the flan caramel:

¾ cup (150 g) white sugar
¼ cup (60 ml) water

For the flan custard:

1 (14-ounce [535 g]) can sweetened condensed milk
1 (12-ounce [360 g]) can evaporated milk (we prefer Carnation)
1¾ cups (420 g) heavy whipping cream
1½ tablespoons (22 g) vanilla extract
5 eggs, room temperature
¼ teaspoon sea salt

Ingredients continued

1. Preheat oven to 350°F (180°C). Create a water bath by using a deep baking dish that is deeper than the flan mold and filling it halfway with hot water.
2. Make the flan caramel: In a small saucepan over medium heat, combine sugar and water. Allow to simmer for 8 to 10 minutes until mixture reaches a dark golden brown color. Do not stir. Remove from heat and pour the caramel mixture into your flan mold, swirling the mold in a circular motion to evenly coat the bottom. Set aside and let cool at room temperature, allowing caramel to harden.
3. Make the flan custard: In a large mixing bowl, whisk together sweetened condensed milk, evaporated milk, heavy whipping cream, vanilla extract, eggs, and sea salt until everything is combined well and smooth. Carefully pour flan custard mixture over hardened caramel in flan mold. Place the flan mold into the water bath. Bake for 1 hour to 1 hour and 20 minutes. Flan is ready when you can tell it has set and the center and surface of the flan is still bouncy. Remove flan mold from water bath and refrigerate for 6-plus hours or overnight.

PRO TIPS:

You will need a 9-inch (23 cm) circular pie or flan mold for this recipe. Also note that you need coconut cream, not coconut milk, for this recipe.

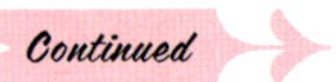

Continued from previous page

For the ginger coconut caramel sauce:

½ cup (100 g) white sugar
2 tablespoons (30 ml) water
¼ cup (35 g) coconut cream
½ tablespoon grated ginger
Pinch salt

4. Make the ginger coconut sauce: In a small saucepan over medium heat, combine sugar and water. Do not stir. Allow to simmer for 8 to 10 minutes until mixture reaches a dark golden brown color. Lower heat to low and slowly whisk in coconut cream. Be careful not to let the mixture splash on you! It will be hot! Slowly stir in grated ginger and salt. Simmer on low heat for 1½ minutes until the sauce has thickened slightly and becomes smooth. Remove from heat and cool for 10 minutes.
5. Before serving, use a knife or small spatula to separate the flan from the outside edges of the flan mold, then carefully flip the flan over onto a serving platter. Serve flan cold and by the slice, drizzled with ginger coconut sauce. Enjoy! This is one of Andrew Ho's favorite desserts!

ACKNOWLEDGMENTS

Andrew Ho. This cookbook could not have happened without so many truly amazing people whom I am blessed to have by my side.

Thank you to my wife, Tabitha, who has been with me from the very beginning of this insane journey. Your love rocks. To our daughter, Amelia, and our English bulldog, Avery, y'all's love and energy keep me going every day.

Huge thanks to our staff and team for all their hard work and dedication and to my family, travel friends, and everyone from Texas, Thailand, Vietnam, and beyond. Your support, starting from way back when this all began as little more than a silly idea, is the reason any of this became real. From the bottom of my heart, I am grateful to have you all along for the ride.

Andrew Samia. Thank you to my beautiful wife, Rachel, who has put up with my nonsense for far too long and reminds me that without love in the dream the dream will never come true. Thank you to my kids, Rowan, Lilly, and Kyren, for forcing me to grow up a bit and for bringing a joy to my life that I never knew was possible. To my parents and in-laws, who instilled a great work ethic in me and never wavered in their unconditional love and support. And to my siblings, who make me so proud to be known as their older brother. I love all of you so much.

To our long-time employees turned family, Brandee, Jesalynn, Grace, Kyla, Colby, Richard, and Rob, thank you for your loyalty and dedication over the years and for trusting the process even when it seems impossible.

I also want to give a shout-out to a good friend and mentor, Chad Carey. Thank you, Chad, for believing in us and helping us get this whole Curry Boys thing started in that tiny pink shack five years ago.

Lastly, I want to thank everyone else who pours their all into Curry Boys BBQ and South BBQ on a daily basis to keep them running. The restaurant industry can be tough, and we truly appreciate everything y'all do to always go above and beyond.

Sean Wen. I have to start by thanking my wonderful partner, Lynnette, who has always supported me, and who has taken time out of her busy day to read my drafts for this book, even when they were a barely coherent mess. I am genuinely so grateful for your unwavering love and support.

I also want to thank my parents, who helped inspire my love of food and are proud of what I do, even if I didn't quite make it into the "doctor, lawyer, or banker" club. It truly means the world to have you two in my corner every single day.

To Ryan, Falcon, and Zach, your friendship and enthusiastic support have given me the motivation to constantly be at my best. Your combined creative inspiration cannot be understated when it comes to my writing and I'm so happy to have you guys in my life.

A big thanks to everyone at Harvard Common Press and Quarto for really believing in this idea, and a special shout-out to Dan Rosenberg, our editorial director, who patiently helped us navigate this wild ride of first-time book writing.

To photographer Eric Pohl and stylist Susan Gebhard, I am so incredibly grateful for the care and attention you poured into making our dishes look absolutely stunning in the book's photographs. This book is beautiful because of you guys!

And lastly, but perhaps most importantly, I want to give a *huge* thank you to our incredible team at Curry Boys BBQ. Major love to our good friend and partner, Adam, holding it down in Nashville. Also, big shout-outs in particular to Grace, Colby, Richard, Kyla, Aaron, and Rob for heroically helping us out during our photo shoots and ensuring we didn't completely drown with all of the other glorious chaos happening in our lives. We are so incredibly lucky to have you all on the team.

ABOUT *the* AUTHORS

Collectively, **Andrew Ho**, **Andrew Samia**, and **Sean Wen** are the Curry Boys. In 2016, Andrew Ho and Sean Wen founded Pinch Boil House and Bia Bar, an Asian street food–themed restaurant in San Antonio, Texas. In 2020, they teamed up with Andrew Samia, San Antonio's best young pitmaster and the chef/owner of South BBQ & Kitchen, to launch Curry Boys BBQ restaurant. Remarkably, within three years, the trio had earned two James Beard Best Chef nominations for Curry Boys BBQ, had appeared on numerous national television BBQ and food shows, and had been featured in *Texas Monthly*, on CNBC, and on many other media outlets. Beyond the two Curry Boys BBQ locations in San Antonio, the Curry Boys opened a third location in Nashville, Tennessee, in early 2025.

Individually, they are:

Andrew Ho. A first-generation Vietnamese American, Andrew's culinary journey is deeply rooted in his family's kitchen and in his extensive travels through Thailand and Vietnam, all of which inspire his unique blend of traditional and innovative flavors.

Andrew Samia. Andrew Samia is a Texas pitmaster and restaurateur with a passion for blending tradition and creativity. Born in New Bedford, Massachusetts, he made his way to Texas as a teenager and, twenty years ago, finally found a true home in San Antonio after falling in love with the food and culture of the city. Andrew is the co-owner and pitmaster of Curry Boys BBQ, where he helped pioneer a Southeast Asian–inspired twist on classic Texas barbecue, and the owner and pitmaster of South BBQ & Kitchen, a barbecue joint rooted in authentic South Texas flavors. Beyond the pit, Andrew's greatest accomplishment is being a husband to his amazing wife, Rachel, and father to their three inspiring children—Rowan, Lilly, and Kyren. When he's not trimming briskets or tending fires, you can find Andrew relaxing with his family near any body of water or camping in Big Bend National Park.

Sean Wen. Born and raised in the Lone Star State, Sean Wen splits his time between working at his restaurant, Curry Boys BBQ, and pondering the twin pillars of his universe: food and basketball. A true disciple of the "Ball Is Life" ethos, you'll often find him shooting hoops at one of the outdoor courts in his current stomping grounds of San Antonio.

The Curry Boys, from left: Andrew Ho, Sean Wen, and Andrew Samia

INDEX

D

E

P

Q

R

S